THIS YEAR'S ASHES
BY JANE BODIE

CURRENCY PRESS
SYDNEY

GRIFFIN THEATRE COMPANY SYDNEY

CURRENCY PLAYS

First published in 2011
by Currency Press Pty Ltd,
PO Box 2287, Strawberry Hills, NSW, 2012, Australia
enquiries@currency.com.au
www.currency.com.au
in association with
Griffin Theatre Company, Sydney.

NATIONAL LIBRARY OF AUSTRALIA CIP DATA
      Author: Bodie, Jane.
      Title: This year's ashes / Jane Bodie.
      ISBN: 9780868199023 (pbk.)
      Series: Current theatre series.
      Dewey Number: A822.4

Typeset by Dean Nottle for Currency Press.
Cover photograph by Michael Corridore. Cover design by Interbrand. Front
cover shows Belinda Bromilow.

Currency Press acknowledges the Traditional Owners of the Country on which
we live and work. We pay our respects to all Aboriginal and Torres Strait
Islander Elders, past and present.

Contents

For my dad.

This Year's Ashes was co-commissioned by Griffin Theatre Company and PlayWriting Australia and was first produced by Griffin Theatre Company at the SBW Stables Theatre, Sydney, on 12 October 2011, with the following cast:

ELLEN	Belinda Bromilow
BRIAN	Tony Llewellyn-Jones
MAN 1 / MAN 2 / ADAM	Nathan Lovejoy

Director, Shannon Murphy
Assistant Director, Brandon Martignago
Designer, Rita Carmody
Lighting Designer, Verity Hampson
Composer, Steve Francis
Sound Designer Nate Edmondson

The play was developed with the support of Mary Wilson and James Emmett.

CHARACTERS

ELLEN, a woman in her mid to late 30s
BRIAN, a man in his early 60s
MAN 1 / MAN 2 / ADAM, to be played by the same actor

A NOTE ON PUNCTUATION

/ indicates the exact point of interruption in overlapping dialogue.

'…' denotes a trailing off.

Omission of a full stop indicates either that the following line of dialogue comes straight in if spoken by another character, or a change of thought or tack mid-dialogue if spoken by the one character.

When a character name is followed by a dash in the place of dialogue (i.e. ELLEN—), it indicates that the character has nothing to say, but should be afforded the length of the unforthcoming answer.

THANKS

My love and thanks to Anthony and Troy, Mark, Sylvia and Lachlan for true friendship in a new place.

And for all things Cricket, humble thanks to TLJ, Sam, Todd and Peter Savage.

This play went to press before the end of rehearsals and may differ from the play as performed.

The play can be performed without an interval. If there is an interval, it should occur between Scenes Six and Seven.

SCENE ONE

In darkness we hear the sound of a MAN *having sex.*

He is loud, seemingly coming.

MAN 1: Oh… God, yeah, yes… yeah fuck… *fuck it... yes!*

He has come.

A short moment of his breathing slowing. Then a bedside light comes on, brighter than we expect.

We are in a bedroom, nondescript. The floor is littered with the occasional pair of socks, underpants. ELLEN *is sitting on the side of the bed with the light on it, her back to the* MAN. *All we can see of what she is wearing is a bra. The bottom part of her body is covered with a section of bedding.*

The MAN *is young, rabbit-like, excitable and damp with sweat. He blinks in the lights, on his elbows, still recovering his breath. He looks over to her.*

That was quick.

ELLEN *doesn't move.*

I mean, that was

ELLEN *begins looking at the floor, searching for an item of her clothing.*

The… light

She locates her skirt on the floor, pulls it on, keeping herself covered.

I didn't mean

That wasn't quick. That was.

Not quick, *at all.*

A beat. She bends down, places her hand under the bed and retrieves a pair of tights, somehow not what she wanted.

Was it?

Pretty sure that one was longer than the first one.

She gets up, scans the room.

I meant the light. My… bedside light. Just… you found it pretty quick

She sees her top on the other side of the room, on the floor, tries to work out if she can make it to it.

Don't reckon I've ever found it that quick, in the dark.

Lived here nearly two years. Never just leaned over, you know and

She decides to attempt walking over to her top.

Actually, it's more like one and a half. Longest I've lived anywhere.

She arrives at her top.

Not counting uni. Still took me a while to get the room with the window, and the floorboards.

She picks the top up off the floor.

Other ones have carpet.

She attempts to put it on.

Jake's room has boards, but they're not polished. Actually, that one has a window.

It's not as easy as she thought.

It's the best room, this one, by far.

Always wanted to live here, this city, and in a place like this.

Beat.

And now, I do.

Her top is now on. The MAN *grins, proud, and then stops.*

You think you'd have to pay more, but it's about waiting your turn. We have rules.

The dishwasher really helps. I wouldn't live anywhere without a dish-washer, now. Now I've experienced the difference.

ELLEN *sees that her shoes are on the other side of the room.*

Broke the moment a bit though.

The light.

Just *bang!*

He laughs, then stops. A beat.

ELLEN: Cold

Light of

Beat.

MAN 1: What?

ELLEN: What?

Beat.

MAN 1: Straight through to the keeper.

He mimes something going over his head.

Na, s'good. Get to see what each other, you know, look like.

She looks at him. He smiles, she doesn't.

Your hair's a bit… at the back

She self-consciously touches the back of her hair, which is a mess of knots. She then resumes looking for the rest of her stuff.

Probably not very good for my carbon fingerprint though.

Should get one of them… new light bulbs. Been meaning to. Just, they're so… ugly. And I don't get why there's like a, a… a

Delay.

It's like, like they're a bit, well, more shit.

Then, saving the planet, doesn't have to be pretty. Probably the point, right?

She decides to put her shoes on.

Though, with the dishwasher, which actually does make things easier, you do use less water.

She looks at her tights, then without putting them on she puts her shoes on.

Then my mum won't get one, 'cause she thinks washing them, by hand, *saves* water.

She looks at him, doesn't know what to say.

Could make you a smoothie.

Blueberry. Though they go the quickest. Even if you hide them under the hummus. Should have a house rule about that.

I could do it with soy? Sometimes I drink soy. And it lasts longer round here.

She scans the room, still looking for something.

[*Nodding*] You should eat something, you look hungry.

She scans the floor again.

You looked hungry. Before.

ELLEN *closes her eyes for a second. She then opens them.*

Can do us a proper breakfast. Women always say they want that, don't they, a man that can cook. Though, you know I can't remember a girl round here who's ever let me watch her eat.

Beat.

ELLEN: I'm not…

MAN 1: You're not really a girl, are you, you're more of a, woman.

Beat.

ELLEN: Hungry.

I'm not

MAN 1: See. Why is that? Reckon we just burned more than a few kilojoules

He laughs.

Eggs?

I can make hash browns. Trick is to squeeze the liquid out of the potatoes. More water than you think in an average potato.

It's not really water, it's more a juice.

Potato juice.

She looks like she's going to be sick.

It was, wasn't it?

Quick?

She has no answer.

You wanna go again? Go for the hat trick. I am *pumped.*

I'll be pumped, in a minute.

Just need to…

ELLEN: It was

She waits out the nausea, until it passes.

Fine.

MAN 1: Yeah… somehow that word doesn't sound as… good as it should.

> *Beat.* ELLEN *looks to the door, then back at him.*

You want a shower?

We got an adjustable shower head.

One's called 'rainforest'.

ELLEN: No.

MAN 1: No, I never used that / one.

ELLEN: I don't, want, a… a shower.

> *Beat.*

MAN 1: Bath?

> *She looks at him—a definite 'no'.*

> *He nods, then goes to get up.*

ELLEN: [*with more force than she means*] Don't.

Please… don't.

> *Beat. He lies back down on his elbows. A beat.*

MAN 1: I was a bit over-excited, that's all.

It's a compliment.

Couldn't stop thinking about it in the cab on the way back.

About what you were gonna do to… then you kept saying what you were going to do to me, I mean fucking hell that's like…

> *She looks away.*

Then I remembered I hadn't changed the sheets on my bed for, I've only got the one set of bedding at the. It's not exactly, a set.

Then that track was on, as you took off your

> *She looks at him.*

That Tool track? And then you've got this… this *smell.*

> *She looks at him.*

What is that?

ELLEN: I have to go.

MAN 1: How old do you think I am?

> *She looks at the door.*

Do you like

She looks back at him.

Tool?

ELLEN: —

MAN 1: Hey, I'm up for just, you know sex, if that's… what you're into, what you're looking for

ELLEN: I'm… looking for my knickers

He laughs, suddenly childish.

MAN 1: Na, it's just a funny word. Like something my mum would say. No, it is something my mum would… fucking great, now I'm talking about my mum again.

Beat.

What do they look like?

Your… knickers?

He has to stop himself from laughing.

ELLEN: I really have to go.

MAN 1: It's the middle of the night.

She looks at her wrist as if for a watch. She isn't wearing one. She touches her wrist—the place where a watch would be worn.

ELLEN: It isn't. Not anymore.

She picks up her bag, puts her tights in it.

MAN 1: You know they say men shouldn't have soy milk, these days. But I like it.

Now I've fucking got used to it.

I think it's better in coffee.

You wanna know my theory on why that is?

ELLEN *looks at him.*

Because it's bean, and bean.

Beat.

ELLEN: Thank you

MAN 1: It's just a theory. Hasn't been proved.

She puts her bag on her shoulder. She looks at him.

You haven't even let me make you breakfast.

ELLEN: I'll

Get... something

At

This word so quiet, she hardly says it:

/ Home.

MAN 1: Yeah? You didn't want to go there last night. Wouldn't tell me where it was.

Thought maybe you were hiding something. Like a, a husband, or

He stops himself.

Did you have a good time?

ELLEN: I don't remember.

MAN 1: Sounded like you did.

Till you went quiet.

I remember every bit. Wrestling sobered me up. Can still feel it in my legs.

You bit me a bit.

She covers her hand with her mouth.

Should I put something on it, it's not bleeding, but I think it broke the / skin.

ELLEN: Why don't you ask your mum?

Beat.

I'm sorry.

MAN 1: I thought that's what people did round here. Have breakfast, talk. Thought they were the rules.

ELLEN: I'm not from here.

MAN 1: What, Stanmore?

You liked me talking last night. Made you laugh. One point your drink came out your nose.

She wipes her face, self-conscious.

Could tell you were sad though. Sitting there on your own, end of the bar.

You kept calling someone, on your phone. But you weren't talking. Just, listening. To something.

You looked sad. In a good way. I mean sad can be hot. Good-looking and sad.

Ugly and sad's a bit...

Who were you calling?

ELLEN: [*sharp*] Look...

> *She wants to say his name, but it's clear she doesn't know it.*

MAN 1: [*reminding her, she knew it last night*] Brian.

> *Beat.*

ELLEN: [*in a whisper*] ... Brian

MAN 1: So, you want my number?

> *Beat.*

Could write it down.

ELLEN: Thing is, I don't want to. I don't want to talk.

> *A moment. He nods.*

MAN 1: I'll look for your...

> *He lies on his stomach on the bed, sticks his head and arms under the bed to search for her knickers.*

Jesus, hope you didn't look down here.

> ELLEN *looks at the door, makes sure she has everything. He goes further under, to retrieve something. She quietly opens the door.*

Reckon this'll be them

> *He sits up, holding a pair of black knickers in his hand like a victory flag, as the door closes. She has gone.*

SCENE TWO

Ellen's flat, morning.

A bare flat. A closed suitcase on the floor, a cheap-looking, non-descript IKEA pouffe—not much else. A door leads to the outside world and a doorway leads to the kitchen. A large window on one wall, with the blind down.

ELLEN *is sitting on the end of her bed. She is wearing the same clothes from the scene before. She stares ahead, occasionally lets out a sob and then stops, as if it hasn't happened. She collects herself. She dials a number on her mobile. Breathes, puts it to her ear.*

BRIAN *silently appears, or is illuminated in the doorway to the kitchen during this, wearing a white, towelling bathrobe. She doesn't notice him at first. He watches her.*

Nobody answers. She waits. The phone then appears to have been answered. She listens. It's not who or what she expected. She listens.

BRIAN: Who you calling?

    ELLEN *turns, startled. She holds the phone in her hand.*

Probably would have picked up by now.

    Beat.

If they were there.

ELLEN: Fucking

    Beat.

Fucking hell.

    BRIAN *steps out into the light.*

BRIAN: What?

ELLEN: You… can't just… fucking, just fucking spring up on me.

BRIAN: There were a lot of *'fuckings'* in that sentence, Ellen.

    Beat.

And I'll have you know I've never sprung up on anyone in my life. I'm not the springing kind.

I'm much more of a *me-anderer.*

    He moves slowly towards her, meanders even, and then stops a little distance away. They look at each other a moment, take each other in.

ELLEN: What are you doing here?

BRIAN: I'm waiting for you to get your breath back. Only fair.

    ELLEN *almost laughs, letting out a single, nervous exhale of breath.*

That's better.

Let me get a proper look at you.

Beat. He goes to step towards her.

ELLEN: Give me a second.

He stops.

Please.

Beat.

How long have you been here?

BRIAN: Not long.

A while

ELLEN: But… how…

BRIAN: How do you think?

She looks at him, not knowing the answer.

Key, under the mat. Els, I've told you about that a thousand times. It's hardly a deterrent, is it? A mat, and one that's so old, it's see-through. I mean, what do I always say?

Beat.

ELLEN: I don't

BRIAN: No, come on, what do I always say?

ELLEN: This isn't Canada.

BRIAN: And why do I say that?

ELLEN: Because… this isn't Canada?

BRIAN: Because, this is the big smoke, kiddo, I could have been anybody breaking in.

ELLEN: You did break in.

BRIAN: *Els*

ELLEN: Don't call me that.

Beat.

BRIAN: I would have phoned, but…

You know what I'm like with mobile phones.

Anyway. Quicker to come visit.

ELLEN: After, two years?

Beat.

BRIAN: Has it been… [two?]

God. Yes, I suppose it has.

Time. Well, it just… you know

Good to see you.

He stops himself. She looks at him, wipes her face, self-conscious.

ELLEN: I must look

BRIAN: You look beautiful. Beautiful Ellen.

Beat.

Your hair's grown.

I like it long.

It's a bit… at the back, it's a bit

ELLEN: [*touching her hair*] What are you doing here?

Beat.

BRIAN: Thought you'd be pleased to see me.

I don't need a reason, do I?

ELLEN: I think under the circumstances you do, yes.

Beat.

BRIAN: I'm just here, Ellen. To see you

Beat.

ELLEN: But why… tonight?

BRIAN: It's not night anymore, not by any stretch of the imagination.

He moves towards the window, where the blind is closed.

Should open this up. Beautiful, the light, this time / of

ELLEN: [*sharp*] No *don't.*

He looks at her. A beat.

BRIAN: Can't I just be here, with you, for a moment?

Beat.

ELLEN: Okay.

That's

It's…

She puts her hand over her mouth, as if about to cry.

BRIAN: It's… alright, kiddo.

> *She nods, silently. A moment.*

Though, you look thin.

> *She pulls a face.*

You're not fat, are you? And your apartment, is a shithole.

> *She laughs, quietly.*

This what they call a *'studio'*?

> *She nods.*

Why do they call it that?

ELLEN: To make it sound artistic.

BRIAN: And, Ellen, please don't tell me that bloody thing's from IKEA.

ELLEN: [*with a laugh*] I can't believe it, that you're here, that you're

BRIAN: I was planning on cooking dinner, surprising you.

ELLEN: Well, you did that.

BRIAN: Then, you weren't home. You don't seem to have a record player. And I couldn't get your TV to work. You haven't even got a bath.

ELLEN: Couldn't afford one, round here.

BRIAN: But you love baths. You used to

ELLEN: There isn't enough room for one in here anyway.

BRIAN: Very artistic.

> *Beat.*

Then I thought I'd do breakfast anyway. To be honest, breakfast is my speciality

ELLEN: It's the only thing you can cook.

BRIAN: There's absolutely nothing in your fridge, Ellen. Not even sure it's on.

ELLEN: It is. There's a bottle of vodka in the freezer.

BRIAN: Well, I was going to bring a bottle of wine. Thought about bringing two.

Then I thought if I brought two, you might think I'd turned into an alcoholic.

ELLEN: Turned into / one?

BRIAN: I'll have you know I don't drink anymore. Not a drop.

Though, not by choice.

And what is that place downstairs, looks like a... massage parlour.

ELLEN: [*with a laugh*] It's a massage parlour.

BRIAN: Good of them to be up-front.

Took me bloody ages to get here.

ELLEN: From where?

Beat.

BRIAN: I could murder a glass of red right now. And a cigarette. Why did I let you make me give up smoking?

ELLEN: I didn't make you.

BRIAN: No.

ELLEN: Where have you been?

Beat.

BRIAN: I was going to ask you the same question. I mean, what time do you call this?

ELLEN: You don't get to ask that.

He nods.

BRIAN: I could comb it for you, if you like.

Get the knots out.

He approaches again. She moves away.

He looks at her, softly.

You look tired.

ELLEN: Thought I looked beautiful.

BRIAN: You do.

But, you're not going to work like that, are you?

ELLEN: I was thinking... maybe I wouldn't go in today.

BRIAN: What? How long have you had that job?

And, why were you crying before?

ELLEN: I need a fucking drink.

She gets up and heads towards the kitchen.

BRIAN: [*calling out*] Not for me, thanks.

He looks at his wrist, a habit, but there is no watch there.

ELLEN *exits.* BRIAN *goes over to her suitcase, thinks about opening it. She re-appears with a large glass of neat vodka and stands in the doorway.*

Liquid breakfast.

She looks at him looking at the suitcase.

Haven't seen this old thing for years.

ELLEN: Can't bring myself to unpack it.

He nods.

I am pleased to see you.

Beat.

BRIAN: So, where have you been tonight then?

He looks at his wrist again.

Last / night.

ELLEN: Out.

BRIAN: [*nodding*] With… friends?

ELLEN: I went to a bar

BRIAN: Oh, anywhere / I'd

ELLEN: And then another bar. And then another, or maybe that was the one before.

BRIAN: Quite a few bars / then

ELLEN: I think maybe there was another one at some point. Couldn't swear by it though, they all look the same after a while. Gay. Then, most of them / are

BRIAN: Big night then, was it? But not with friends?

ELLEN: I don't have any friends, not in Sydney. Not outside of work.

Not, at work.

BRIAN: Well, if you never go in to the place.

Take you a bit of time to settle in, that's all.

ELLEN: I've been here almost two years.

He looks at her closed suitcase and then back at her.

BRIAN: I never imagined you living on your own.

ELLEN: I'm not on my own.

I share the apartment with a family of cockroaches. And it's a very large family.

ELLEN *exits into the kitchen. She comes back with the bottle of vodka and stands in the doorway.*

BRIAN: So what else is new, kiddo?

ELLEN: [*taking a swig*] I'm supposed to prepare for this… presentation, at work.

BRIAN: You'd be good at that. *Presenting.*

ELLEN: Everyone, at work, has to do it. By the end of the month, we all have to present our ideas, to the whole company, and the CEO.

BRIAN: No pressure then.

ELLEN: We have to talk about what… brought us to Sydney and what we, left behind. What we, miss.

It's one of those… team-bonding exercises, but of course it leads to a pitch, it's all about *the pitch.* The product.

BRIAN: Of course

ELLEN: Because there's no reason to leave things behind anymore, to miss anyone, because now we can stay in touch, be in touch, at all times.

She's lost him.

Mobile technology, means nobody need ever miss anybody again.

BRIAN: Unless you lose your phone.

ELLEN: Yes, at which point, we introduce, the product.

BRIAN: Which is…?

ELLEN: A thing you put on your keys, your key ring, that finds your mobile phone.

BRIAN: Howzat?

ELLEN: [*he won't get it*] It, beeps, the two are… linked up, through a, a chip, so the key ring makes the phone beep. If you can't find your phone, you just push a button and it, it finds you. It's going to be iPhone compatible, of course.

BRIAN: [*not knowing what this means*] Of course.

ELLEN: So nobody need ever lose their phone again.

BRIAN: It's genius, Ellen, obviously. Except if you lose your keys.

ELLEN: That's what I said.

It's, the beginning…

BRIAN: … of the end.

Beat.

ELLEN: We've got this launch, couple of weeks. Each of us has to come up with a name for it, something catchy. And they'll choose the best one. It's for this big client, they're spending loads of money on the launch, serving real champagne, whole *shebang*.

BRIAN: [*nodding*] Come up with any names yet?

ELLEN: [*shaking her head*] The… 'i… am… not lost'.

The… 'i am over here'

He laughs and joins in.

BRIAN: The… 'i am bloody over here where you left me last night'.

She laughs with him, then stops.

ELLEN: You know what today is, don't you?

It's the First Test, the first day.

Of the Ashes.

Beat.

BRIAN: Is it?

ELLEN: Come on, I know wherever you went, wherever you've been, you'd know that.

He smiles at her.

We could watch it together.

Beat.

We don't have to

BRIAN: Well, seeing as you've decided you're not even bothering to go into work

ELLEN: I don't have a flat screen.

BRIAN: I've no idea what that means.

She looks at him. He grins.

Personally, I still think you get the best coverage on the wireless.

ELLEN: And how could I go into work?

> *Beat.*

Now you're here.

BRIAN: Well, if we must.

ELLEN: It'll be perfect.

I'll just… get out of these things… freshen up.

BRIAN: I wish you would.

ELLEN: [*beginning to exit*] Make yourself at home.

> ELLEN *exits excitedly.*

> BRIAN *wanders over to the pouffe, inspects it with a look of distaste, and shakes his head. He goes to her bed, which is unmade. He then makes it, carefully straightening each corner.*

> *During this,* ELLEN *comes and stands in the doorway, in a towel, and watches him. He finishes, runs a hand over the top sheet, something tender in it.*

Hospital corners.

BRIAN: That *was* very quick.

ELLEN: Somebody's nicked my bathrobe.

And I wanted to make sure you were still here.

> *Beat.*

You are.

BRIAN: Yes.

ELLEN: You're here.

BRIAN: In your studio.

> *Beat.*

ELLEN: How long are you staying for?

BRIAN: Depends how we do in the cricket.

ELLEN: *Dad.*

> *Beat.*

BRIAN: You need to learn to relax, kiddo.

Just, breathe. And relax.

> *Pause.*

ELLEN: I've dreamt about this moment, I mean actually dreamed it. Of you, just walking in, like this. Of what you'd say, and what I'd do.

BRIAN: And…?

ELLEN: You're not usually in my bathrobe.

BRIAN: And what do I say?

ELLEN: You apologise for leaving, for leaving / me

BRIAN: I didn't leave you.

ELLEN: And then you say that you've wanted to come back before, but you'd got lost.

And you felt like an idiot, for getting lost, so you couldn't come back. But that you wanted to come back and say that.

> *Beat.*

BRIAN: And what do you do?

ELLEN: It changes. Sometimes I tell you that I've dreamt of this moment. And then I say that's it's alright, it doesn't matter now. Because you're back.

> *Beat.*

BRIAN: I have that dream too.

ELLEN: Thought you didn't dream.

BRIAN: For some reason, I do now.

ELLEN: What happens, in your dream?

BRIAN: I look at you.

And I say

Els, please don't tell me that bloody thing's from IKEA.

> *She looks away from him.*

> *He begins to walk towards her and then stops.*

You look about twelve standing there like that.

> *She walks across the room and sits on the end of the bed, facing the TV. She pats the space beside her on the bed.*

ELLEN: Best seat in the house.

> *He sits down beside her on the end of the bed.*

I don't often have guests. Actually, I never have them.

BRIAN: You do now.

He turns to the TV, or it could be her laptop, propped up somehow.

Funny-looking wireless.

ELLEN: [*ignoring him*] It doesn't kick off for two hours.

BRIAN: It doesn't... 'kick off' at all

Play starts. We refer to it as 'the start of play'.

ELLEN: Well, I like to watch the beginning, to go over the rules.

BRIAN: Not rules, Ellen.

Traditions.

He's in the zone.

And of course England will win the toss.

And, they'll choose to bat, because they always choose to bat at The Gabba. But then that's because Harmison can't bowl for his fucking life.

He laughs derisively.

Though, with Strauss up first

He sees her looking at him.

What?

ELLEN: I just. I had this idea of you, this perfect... image of you, wherever you were, watching it.

BRIAN: That's nice.

ELLEN: It made me sad.

Beat.

BRIAN: I'm sorry.

I'm sorry, Els.

ELLEN: It's alright.

Beat.

It doesn't matter now.

She smiles at him, then points the remote at the TV and presses 'on'. The match preamble to the First Test begins to play.

They watch it for a moment, then the lights begin to fade.

In the darkness we hear highlights of the first day of play.

SCENE THREE

A new bedroom. Different from either of the ones we have seen, both bed and position of the door have now changed. The room is also neater, more Sydney.

A MAN *enters. He is bare-chested, in boxers, and carrying two cups. He seems older than* MAN 1, *surer of himself, and moves with more weight and purpose, almost a swagger. He enters the room as if he expects someone else to be in his bed. He looks at the bed and sees that it's empty. He takes this information in for a second and then sits on the bed. He looks behind him at the shape left on the other side of the bed.*

He takes a sip from one of the cups; it isn't what he expected. He then takes a sip from the other, and is slightly more satisfied, though not entirely. He breathes out. He tries to scratch his balls with an elbow, without putting down either of the cups. He then puts one down and has a good scratch. He sees a mobile phone on the floor by the bed. He picks it up, looks at it.

There is a knock on his door, quiet at first. He looks to the door, doesn't move.

Another knock, louder this time. He puts the phone down and goes to the door. He opens it. ELLEN *stands there. A beat.*

ELLEN: Hi

MAN 2: Thought you'd gone.

ELLEN: No.

I was

He turns his back on her and walks into his room.

I was going to

MAN 2: Right.

ELLEN *enters the room.*

Didn't know whether you wanted coffee or tea. So I made one of each. Even got the plunger out.

ELLEN: Thanks, but

MAN 2: So. What do you want?

ELLEN: —?

MAN 2: Tea?

Or, coffee?

He holds his cup out.

ELLEN: No, thanks

MAN 2: Now that's a mixed message. I say tea, or coffee, and you, you're supposed to tell me which one you prefer, right now. Actually, is that a mixed message?

Beat. She smiles.

ELLEN: Tea.

MAN 2: I would have said you were a coffee girl.

But that's good.

He holds out the tea, smiles.

Keep me on my toes

She takes the cup, sits on his bed with him.

ELLEN: I didn't know where I was, when I woke up.

MAN 2: Woollahra

ELLEN: No, I mean.

I went out into the street

MAN 2: Hot out there?

ELLEN: Yes.

MAN 2: You look hot.

Was hoping you'd come and join me, in the shower. I tried waking you up. You were making noises, you know, like you were awake, like you wanted to be. But then I couldn't get any sense out of you. You were all-out, dead, to the world.

I had a cold shower.

Beat.

Already hot again now. What about you?

ELLEN: I'm... okay

MAN 2: Hoped you'd hang round, give me a reason to go back to bed.

But it's cool, I got shit to do too, yeah.

ELLEN: Yeah.

MAN 2: So why'd you come back?

    Beat.

ELLEN: [*quietly*] I left my, my… phone

MAN 2: What?

ELLEN: I'm not sure if it's

    He starts to laugh.

MAN 2: That is, [*laughing*] come on, that is pretty funny.

You spend half the night telling everyone, convincing us all that life isn't worth living without, one of… those things, that you wouldn't be seen dead without one. I thought you had the thing stapled to your hand.

And now you've gone and lost your. You've got to admit that is pretty funny

ELLEN: Yeah, I think it might hurt, to… laugh.

    He laughs, softens. So does she. She smiles.

MAN 2: Thought the real shit wasn't supposed to give you a hangover.

ELLEN: Yeah.

MAN 2: That's if it really was the real shit.

You know, I was gonna get online this morning and order one of the things for myself, before they sold out, site's probably crashing by now

ELLEN: I don't think so

MAN 2: No, what I'm saying is you did a good job, we were all frothing at the mouth about the things, wondering how we'd ever survived without one.

ELLEN: I was just, doing my job

MAN 2: Pretty good job, I reckon. Making people buy shit they don't need.

    Beat.

ELLEN: Actually, it's a good product. Company know what they're doing, the mark-up isn't even that big

MAN 2: Why haven't you got one then, things are so fucking good?

Beat.

ELLEN: It's a job.

It's my job to make you... feel

MAN 2: What?

ELLEN: To make you feel you want, need, whatever it is we're, selling.

MAN 2: And you did that, last night. So you should be pleased with yourself.

ELLEN: Yeah.

MAN 2: You don't look very pleased with yourself.

ELLEN: I'm just

I don't make a habit of

Of

MAN 2: Finishing your own sentences?

ELLEN: Going home with people from work.

MAN 2: I'm not from your work. I was an invited guest, client.

ELLEN: There are, rules, that's all.

MAN 2: I bet there are. Bet you've broken more than a few.

ELLEN: [*getting up*] I should look for my

MAN 2: What are they then?

Beat.

The rules?

I want to know if I played along, played the game.

Beat.

Who's winning?

Reckon you were probably in front, last night, when we got them to re-open the tab. That was when you had us all, captive audience. Half of us didn't know what our own names were by then, but we all wanted one of whatever you were selling.

Not sure you made all the other clients feel as well looked after as me, but you had me eating out of the palm of your hand.

ELLEN: I think I probably left it around the bed.

MAN 2: What's it called again?

He is close to her now.

ELLEN: The… 'i am still here'

    Beat.

MAN 2: You are hot. Can feel it from here. Can smell it. What is that?

ELLEN: I'm not / really

MAN 2: I could go another one, right now. A shower.

    Scrub your back. Soap up your

    Get those knots out of your hair.

ELLEN: I really… have to

MAN 2: You've got that down to a tee, haven't you? The lost… vulnerable bit. Different story last night. Thought you were going to rip my fucking tongue out.

    Beat.

ELLEN: I'm… sorry

    He's as close as he can get.

MAN 2: Sorry you licked blood out of my mouth, or sorry you sobered up?

    Somehow he is stopping her from moving.

    You should have another drink. Your fucking eyes are wild.

ELLEN: I really… would like

MAN 2: What?

    What you looking at me like that for? Like I've changed all of a sudden. That's you, babe.

    That part of the game?

    Because I have to say I thought you'd be up for more than three goes, eyes like that. What's that… three strikes and you're out?

    He laughs.

ELLEN: [*loud*] I really *do need my phone!*

    Beat.

MAN 2: Yeah, well I'd recommend a solution for that, but you already know about it. You just didn't buy one, which I have to say isn't a huge fucking vote of confidence.

    And probably means I'm now in the lead. If we're still playing.

    Beat.

Why don't you try and whistle for it, your phone?

Like a dog.

He is close, almost touching her. The sound is still growing.

You really need to relax

ELLEN: Please stop

MAN 2: What?

ELLEN: Stop

MAN 2: You look about twelve right now.

ELLEN: Brian, please get out of *my face!*

He steps back, his hands up.

MAN 2: Oh, that is fucking

I thought your novelty fucking key ring was a bit steep, but you are fucking priceless.

ELLEN: I'm sorry.

MAN 2: *Tom,* I'm sorry, Tom.

Your phone's just there. By the bed. Where you left it.

Neither of them move. He walks over to the phone, holds it out.

Here you go.

She reaches and takes the phone. The sound is now quite loud.

Do I get yours?

Your name?

That another rule?

ELLEN: I'm leaving now. I'm

MAN 2: Yeah.

Beat.

Go on then.

Beat.

Go.

She leaves.

SCENE FOUR

Ellen's apartment, lunchtime.

BRIAN *is standing beside the bed, some space has been cleared and a few bits of furniture have been re-arranged, to give a sense of a cricket pitch, with key player positions, stumps, et cetera.*

BRIAN *is holding a rolled-up newspaper as a bat and* ELLEN *is standing, trying to look like she's fielding. We sense that* BRIAN *has gone over this a few times. The radio cricket coverage is playing quietly in the background.*

BRIAN: So. That's Strauss at first, Swann on second, and Collingwood on third.

ELLEN: Got it.

BRIAN: Three slips, yes, and a gully. Point, mid off

ELLEN: Mid on.

BRIAN: Yes. Off side, on side, right and left. Mid wicket, and deep cover point. Yeah?

> ELLEN *laughs.*

What?

ELLEN: Nothing. I just. You said that. Deep cover point.

No, this is fun.

BRIAN: [*deadly serious*] And then there's fine leg.

ELLEN: And, not forgetting silly point. And where's Alastair Cook?

> *Beat.*

BRIAN: What?

ELLEN: The one, with the eyes.

BRIAN: [*rolling his eyes*] Ellen, bit of focus.

> *He bangs the rolled-up newspaper on the floor, as if it's a bat.*

ELLEN: Told you this would be perfect.

BRIAN: Mn?

ELLEN: This, it's perfect.

BRIAN: *Crucial*, it's… a crucial point in the Test, yes, but it's hardly perfect, Ellen.

ELLEN: We beat them at Adelaide though, 2006, by six wickets.

BRIAN: Yeah, it's not

ELLEN: And I know Strauss says he's 'happy with the way they're play-ing', but England would want to be a bit, wary. And, now we've got Bollinger.

BRIAN: Sometimes, Ellen, you make me a very proud father.

Now, where are you standing?

ELLEN: Mid wicket.

BRIAN: You'd be better off at first slip.

She moves.

First, slip.

She's not sure where to go.

You're at third man and you're never going to catch the bloody ball there.

ELLEN: I know I'm / not

BRIAN: Not at third man, you're not, no.

ELLEN: We're standing in my apartment, Dad.

BRIAN: Your, studio.

ELLEN: Dad, we haven't even got a ball.

Beat.

BRIAN: Use your imagination, Ellen. You used to be good at that.

She looks at him. She swats the air to create a breeze.

Don't swat those flies, Jardine, they're the only friends you've got.

He laughs, amused by himself.

Why don't you open the window, let some air in?

ELLEN: Because it's thirty-five degrees out there.

Come on, I'm ready

BRIAN: You don't look ready.

You look

ELLEN: [*ignoring him*] So, the batsman calls it.

BRIAN: He calls. Not 'it', he doesn't call 'it', he just

ELLEN: The batsman 'calls'

BRIAN: If he hits it in front of square. If the ball goes behind, the batsman at the non-striker's end calls.

ELLEN: And why is it called that again?

BRIAN: What?

ELLEN: Silly point.

BRIAN: You've got deep long, short and silly.

ELLEN: Why?

BRIAN: In relation to how close you are to the batsman

ELLEN: What's... silly about that?

BRIAN: Come closer to me, and I'll bloody show you.

> *He looks at her.*

Ellen, do you want to go over this, I thought you got it.

ELLEN: I do. Basically.

BRIAN: Basically?

ELLEN: Yeah. The basics.

BRIAN: The, 'basics'.

ELLEN: Yes.

BRIAN: Basically, Ellen, there are two sides. One out in the field, and one in. Basically.

> *She is about to protest, but he continues.*

Each man that's in the side that's in, goes out. And when he's out, he comes in and the next man goes in. Until he's, basically out.

ELLEN: Yeah / okay

BRIAN: Then when they are all out, the side that's out comes in and the side that's been in goes out and tries to get those coming in, out.

Occasionally you get men still in and not out. When a man goes out to go in, the men who are out try to get him out, and when he is out he goes in and the next man in goes out and goes in.

There are two men called umpires, who stay out all the time and they decide when the men who are in are out.

Then, when both sides have been in and all the men have been given out, and both sides have been out twice after all the men have been in, including those who are not out, then and only then, the game is, basically, over.

Get it?

ELLEN: —

BRIAN: There is nothing basic about cricket, Ellen. It's… it's a chess match, not a fucking shit fight.

Beat.

ELLEN: You said you didn't mind. Showing / me.

BRIAN: I don't.

Of course I

I love this.

You, me

ELLEN: Silly point.

Beat.

So, we're now three wickets down.

BRIAN: Indeed we are.

ELLEN: Which is bad.

BRIAN: It's more than fucking bad, it's a fucking disaster.

ELLEN: There was a lot of 'fuckings' in that sentence, Brian.

She's amused, he's not.

Wait. Hang on a minute…

She goes to the suitcase, opens it carefully, and pulls out a cricket bat. She closes it. She hands the bat to him, stays close. He inspects it, lovingly.

BRIAN: [*admiring it, lost for a moment*] Ah. The old… thwack of leather on willow.

ELLEN: [*proud*] I oiled it.

BRIAN: Did you? [*Frowning*] With what?

ELLEN: [*sarcastic*] Vegemite.

Beat.

BRIAN: I'm glad you kept it.

ELLEN: Mum didn't want it.

Beat. She assumes the position.

So… Watson.

You were… explaining, the problem with

BRIAN: The tragedy, Ellen, the fucking tragedy with Shane Watson, is. He runs

ELLEN: Thought that was the idea.

BRIAN: Yes, but Watson, runs people out.

She's still not getting it.

Watson obviously has talent, but he lacks the right… temperament, attitude. He's your new breed, Y Gen, ear stud, vitamin ads, *ridiculous* hair. These poor fucks are all manicured within an inch of their lives, when what they need is to be putting in time at the nets.

And worse, he's in a rush. Poor kid wants to run

ELLEN: Because he wants to score

BRIAN: Yes, but at who's expense, Ellen?

It's the first day of the Second Test, yeah? There's still four days, four long days, stages, of this Test to go. Kid needs to wait.

She looks at him, wanting to understand.

You've got to get your eye in first, take it easy, watch the rush of blood.

First you've got to think, then you can feel, *feel* your way into the game, because that's how you stay in, how you stay, alive.

She looks at him.

ELLEN: And here's me, thinking it's just a load of blokes standing around in white.

He looks at her exasperated.

And Shane Warne has ridiculous hair.

Beat.

BRIAN: I'm not even going / to

ELLEN: Implants. And he's had his teeth capped.

BRIAN: It's… irrelevant how he… the man is a god.

ELLEN: A bright orange god, with hair plugs, who's now / shagging

BRIAN: Shane Warne, at his peak, was one of the greatest bowlers in the history of the game, possibly *the* greatest.

She's not convinced. He takes a serious breath.

The perfect spin ball is a thing of great beauty, Ellen.

He takes an apple from her fruit bowl. He spins the apple with his fingers. She nods, not really getting it, but involved anyway.

It all rests on the orientation of the seam. So you've got your fast bowling, using the seam, and the swing. And then spin. Wrist, or finger.

And then of course you've got the *wrong-un*.

ELLEN: Right.

BRIAN: And the flipper.

ELLEN: And which did Warne do? Which one of / those

BRIAN: Shane Warne could do all of them, every one, perfectly executed. But the beauty of his bowling, the brilliance, was that whatever the *Sheik of Tweak* was bowling, he'd make it look like he was doing one of the others.

ELLEN: But that's, that's cheating.

BRIAN: What?

ELLEN: Looking like, you're gonna do one thing and then doing another, it's, lying.

BRIAN: Sounds remarkably similar to marketing.

ELLEN: How do you do that?

How can you justify that, talking about it, like it's somehow… better, it's this thing that's beyond the rules of everything else.

BRIAN: Because it is.

Everything else these days, is… TV, might as well be. But cricket, at its best, is pure theatre.

The Ashes defines summer, Ellen, defines, where each country stands. It defines who we are. If we understand it.

ELLEN: It's still lying.

She takes the apple out of his hand and bites into it.

BRIAN: What I don't understand is why you bother watching it, if you don't get it.

Beat. ELLEN *exits to the kitchen.*

BRIAN *looks towards the door, the space she's made. A moment.*

*He then goes over and fiddles with the radio, which has the sound
down low. He looks to the kitchen and turns the radio up. He holds
it to his ear, then puts it on the table.*

[*Calling out*] Back on in a minute.

ELLEN *comes back into the room.*

ELLEN: The cockroaches have gone.

BRIAN: Yes, well eventually even cockroaches need food to survive.

Beat.

I'm sorry.

ELLEN: It's fine.

BRIAN: It isn't.

Beat.

It's possibly Australia's worst start to a match in one hundred and
thirty-three years of Test-match cricket on day one of the Second Test,
is what it is.

ELLEN: Could be worse.

BRIAN: How?

ELLEN: I could be watching it on my own.

You could be.

Beat.

BRIAN: Yes.

Sorry.

ELLEN: What happens if we lose?

He looks at her.

Are you going to

BRIAN: There are still nineteen days to go, nineteen glorious days. That's
the beauty of it, the essential nature of the five-Test Series.

And it ain't over yet, kiddo, not by a long chalk.

He walks towards her, as if he is going to touch her, and then stops.

You've got to have some faith. Both of us, need to have faith.

And you really need to relax.

The lights fade.

SCENE FIVE

In the darkness we hear a sharp intake of breath, as ELLEN *gasps, cries out in her sleep. She sits up, reaches for the light, hits it hard, and we hear it break.*

Lights come up, dimly. We are in Ellen's apartment. ELLEN *is in exactly the same position as she was in the first scene, and there is a man,* ADAM, *beside her. He too should be almost in exactly the same position as* MAN 1 *from the first scene.*

ADAM *sits up on his elbows.* ELLEN *looks slightly stunned.*

ADAM: Too fast.

> ELLEN *doesn't move.*

Too hard

> ELLEN *closes her eyes, rubs her face with both hands.*

And too quick.

> *With her eyes only half open,* ELLEN *assumes her side-of-the-bed position, with her back to him. She slowly reaches down and looks for her clothes, or just something that tells her she's alive.*
> *She finds something—looks like a pair of her knickers, but she's not sure.*

The light.

> *She gulps.*

Hit it too hard and too fast.

> *She finds a t-shirt and pulls it over her head.*

Did the old alarm clock reflex, the *snooze slap*, but you did it with the light. Not the same thing.

> *She half turns to him, half closes her eyes.*

You… / alright?

ELLEN: I'm fine.

> *He nods.*

ADAM: Because I think we drunk a bit

More than a bit. And I'm pretty sure we ended up at the Judgement Bar. Which is, ironic. That was the last place I remember, after the Iguana Bar. After the Pyrmont Bridge Hotel.

And I don't think we got much sleep.

He pulls out his glasses.

Though I slept on these.

He puts them on, they're wonky.

Actually, I don't feel so bad.

He grins. She doesn't move. He takes his glasses off, looks slightly sketchy.

Maybe we should

ELLEN: No.

ADAM: What?

ELLEN: I don't want a

    Beat.

ADAM: What?

ELLEN: Shower.

ADAM: Me neither.

    Beat.

ELLEN: I don't want. Anything.

ADAM: Okay.

  I wasn't really

  Okay

    He goes to get up.

ELLEN: No, don't, *don't!*

  Please

  I'm sorry.

    Beat.

  I'm sorry, about the lamp.

ADAM: It's your lamp.

    Beat.

ELLEN: What?

She looks over at the lamp.

ADAM: They should be apologising. The lamp / company

ELLEN: No, no that's

She starts looking around the room, only now taking it in. She realises that she is, in fact, in her own room.

ADAM: For making such a cheap, shitty, bedside lamp, that masquerades as an alarm clock, in the dark. You could have had your eye out.

ELLEN: I...

ADAM: IKEA?

She looks at him, frightened.

The lamp, I bet it's from

He looks at her realising that she is not alright.

ELLEN *suddenly exits into the kitchen.*

ADAM *waits for a second and then gets up. He is naked. As he stands, he feels quite a bit worse than he expected.*

ELLEN *comes back in, still looking frightened.* ADAM *grabs a pillow and covers his groin.*

Still there?

ELLEN: What?

ADAM: Your kitchen?

Beat.

Think we finished your vodka, though. No. We definitely did. I washed up your glasses.

She looks at the pillow.

You lost something?

You look, like you've

ELLEN: I thought...

ADAM: What?

Beat.

ELLEN: In the kitchen... there was

Did you, see

ADAM: Dead.

> *Beat.*

I killed it. Big fucker too. Made this noise, when I

> *He mimes squashing the cockroach. She looks back at the kitchen door, then back at him.*

Hey, it's alright

ELLEN: It isn't.

> *Beat.*

It isn't.

I'm sorry.

> *Beat.*

ADAM: You know, you say that a lot.

You don't need to. You've got nothing to be sorry about. Not to me anyway.

Though, I'm pretty sure it was you, broke my glasses.

And the lamp.

> *She looks back at the kitchen door, then back at him.*

And that's my t-shirt. One you've got on.

> *Beat. She comes over, sits on the bed with her back to him. She takes the t-shirt off, without turning. She holds it out. He takes it. He looks at her naked back for a moment. He puts the t-shirt on, but keeps the pillow there. She finds something on the floor and puts it on. It covers her. She stands up.*

My turn.

ELLEN: What?

> *Beat.*

ADAM: There'd be a view out there, wouldn't there? Out that window.

> *She looks to the window.*

Bet it's beautiful this time of morning. This light. Could almost see the water from here, couldn't you?

[*Holding up his glasses*] Well I couldn't, but

ELLEN: Don't know.

ADAM: If you stood on a chair maybe. At an angle.

What angle would you have to stand at to see the water, see Elizabeth Bay from here. Or is this officially Elizabeth Bay?

ELLEN: I'm not… I'm not sure what you're asking.

ADAM: I was, trying to… distract you.

I can't find my jocks

She looks at the pillow. She laughs, suddenly, covers her mouth with a hand.

Pretty sure I left them… somewhere round here.

He almost drops the pillow. Grabs it, holds onto it tight.

Can't have gone far.

He looks, then stops.

And, I think I've got an erection.

Actually, I'm pretty sure it's going now.

Though sometimes it, it's a good thing. Well, in a situation that calls for one, for an erect…

Is this an Egyptian cotton?

She nods.

Yeah, you can feel the quality. Soft.

He checks under the pillow.

Yep.

She looks at him.

I'll

He starts looking around the flat for his jocks, his other clothes, holding the pillow in place. She watches him as he retrieves them, one by one.

Yeah, definitely a bit hung-over

He finds his jocks. He stands with the pillow still against him, trying to negotiate putting them on. She watches. He motions for her to look away.

Do you… mind?

She half looks away. He then decides to sit on the bed, his back to her, and slides them on, some attempt at delicacy, modesty. She watches. He stands.

He gets his jeans, starts putting them on, manages to unbalance himself and fall over, somewhat spectacularly. She laughs.

He gets up and tries again, this time succeeding. She watches. He puts his glasses on. He looks at her.

ELLEN: They're a bit

Your… glasses, they're a bit

She motions that they're wonky. He tries to straighten them. He looks through them.

ADAM: That hasn't helped.

She laughs, covers her mouth.

You shouldn't do that.

Beat.

Cover it up.

She takes her hand away from her mouth. She breathes. They look at each other.

That's better.

He sees something behind her.

He's back.

She turns around, jumpy.

Some fuckers can't take a hint.

He grabs at a cricket bat that is leaning up against a chair, scans the floor.

ELLEN: No, don't

ADAM: Time to die

ELLEN: Can you not

He swings the bat, still studying the floor for the cockroach.

ADAM: I must be the only bloke round here that doesn't follow the cricket. Only straight bloke. My father's devastated. Haven't got the heart to tell him I was doing a Pilates mat class during the first game.

ELLEN: [*correcting him, sharp*] Test.

> *She holds her hand out for the bat.*

Can you give me / the

ADAM: Though right now it's unavoidable, isn't it? Couldn't avoid it, if you wanted to. And even I know you wouldn't want to be batting for our side right now.

> *She's still holding her hand out. He swings the bat.*

I mean we are getting *smashed*, aren't we?

ELLEN: It's the Ashes.

ADAM: *Killed*

ELLEN: [*louder than she means*] It's a five-Test Series, each match lasts five days. It's the Second Test. We're two Tests in. We've still got three Tests to go, that's fifteen days, fifteen long days.

It still could be anybody's.

> *Beat.*

ADAM: Right. So, are you like a, a fan?

> *She holds out her hand once more.*

ELLEN: Can I

ADAM: You don't look like one, not your average fan.

ELLEN: Yeah, well nothing ends up looking like you think it's going to round here.

I mean, the Opera House, it's tiled.

ADAM: Yeah

ELLEN: I never knew that, until I saw it, up close. Then in this city, everything looks different, up close.

ADAM: That why you broke my glasses?

> *Beat. She holds out her hand for the bat.*

Actually, I thought your flat would look, I don't know, different somehow.

You've lived here a while now, haven't you?

> *She stops, looks at him, confused.*

ELLEN: What?

He bats one of his socks across the room, raises his arms up.

ADAM: *Six!*

He looks at her. A beat.

You don't remember me, do you?

From before. Before last night. We've met before.

It's clear she doesn't remember.

Last night I thought you were just playing… cool. And this morning, I'm like, 'course she knows who I am, why else would she

But you really don't, do you?

Beat.

ELLEN: You do look…

Familiar

ADAM: My… name?

She looks uncomfortable.

Went out with Eve.

Ate an apple

ELLEN: —

ADAM: You could try saying sorry now maybe.

She looks at him.

ELLEN: You should probably go.

Beat.

ADAM: Because… you can't remember my name?

ELLEN: Because, I have things I need to do

ADAM: Hey, I didn't mean

ELLEN: And because I'm expecting somebody.

ADAM: [*looking at his watch*] What, now?

ELLEN: Yes.

ADAM: What is he, a garbo?

Beat.

ELLEN: He'll be here any minute.

ADAM: Bit of a… sticky wicket.

ELLEN: Please just… go.

Beat. He hands her the bat.

ADAM: Mind if I put my other shoe on?

He walks to his shoe, picks it up and puts it on. He is upset.

ELLEN: It's not… it's not you.

It's

I just… I want to be on my own.

ADAM: Thought you had someone coming round.

He looks at her, angry now for the first time.

ELLEN: You got what you wanted, didn't you?

I mean, I didn't say come back to mine and talk. And I'm sure I was explicit about what we were coming back here for. So I haven't lied to you, or asked for anything that you didn't expect

ADAM: You haven't asked me for anything.

ELLEN: So when did such a simple exchange of needs, become so… complicated?

Beat. He goes to leave.

ADAM: [*at the door*] You know, you shouldn't do that. Make out you're alone, if you're not. Because you do it really well. Had me convinced.

And I didn't get what I wanted.

I was really pleased to see you, last night. There you were, on the dance floor. Though you didn't want to dance.

I came back here with you because you wanted me to, and because I I wanted to get to know you better. So, I didn't get what I wanted actually, Ellen.

She looks at him.

You told me it last time. For some reason I remembered.

Beat. ADAM *leaves.*

ELLEN: [*shouting to the door after he has left*] Why do you always do that?

All you… men here.

You just, talk.

ADAM *leaves.* ELLEN *sits on the end of the bed. A moment. She sobs.*

SCENE SIX

We hear select highlights of the Third Test from the radio, in blackout. Lights come up. The flat is now tidier. BRIAN *is lying on Ellen's bed with the radio in his lap. He lies still, eyes closed. The radio plays quietly.*

ELLEN *enters from the kitchen in her bathrobe, eating popcorn from a large bowl. She stops when she sees* BRIAN *lying there.*

ELLEN: Dad?

BRIAN: [*waking with a start*] What?

What did I miss?

ELLEN: [*smiling, relieved*] Nothing.

He fiddles with the radio, turns it up a bit, listens.

BRIAN: [*more to the radio than her*] Notice the Barmy Army have stopped singing now? Gone back to their bloody backpackers' to apply some After-Sun.

She watches him a moment.

ELLEN: I should probably go into work.

At some point

BRIAN: Hm?

ELLEN: Not because I want to.

He looks back at her.

Though I'm out of vodka

BRIAN: Don't look at me.

ELLEN: And this is the last of the popcorn.

BRIAN: Now, that is a balanced diet.

ELLEN: I'll have you know I popped this myself.

BRIAN: Sorry… hang on a minute.

He listens a second.

ELLEN: Anyway, I should just, you know, show my face. Before they forget what I look like.

BRIAN: Amazed they remember now.

He fiddles with the radio, trying to tune it. She comes and sits beside him.

ELLEN: Do we have to listen to the highlights?

BRIAN: You don't have to.

And we are at a pretty important point, in the Series

ELLEN: Thought it was all important.

He looks at her.

And now that we're winning.

Beat.

BRIAN: Yeah, we're not exactly… / winning

ELLEN: But now we've won one Test each.

BRIAN: It's not… we're still fragile, Ellen, our… batting order is still fragile. Do you understand what that means?

ELLEN: / Yes.

BRIAN: [*almost to the radio*] I mean, what the hell does Pup think he's doing… man's gone… AWOL. And as for bloody *Huss*

ELLEN: Why do you give them all names?

BRIAN: What?

ELLEN: The players, you give them… nicknames.

BRIAN: Ours, yes. We only give *our* boys

ELLEN: Except they're not yours, are they, Dad? They're not friends, or… family. You don't even know them.

Beat.

BRIAN: I don't make the rules, Ellen.

ELLEN: Thought they were traditions.

She holds out the bowl to him. He shakes his head. She takes the bowl back.

Yeah, well I should still probably go into work.

BRIAN: I'll be fine.

ELLEN: Somehow that word doesn't sound as good as it should.

He turns and looks at her.

BRIAN: I always loved this city. I… thought you'd feel the same.

ELLEN: Sorry.

BRIAN: Your mother and I always loved it here, loved coming here together.

He laughs.

This was before mini-breaks even existed. She always said the whole city smelled of… sex, that it oozed

ELLEN: Not sure I need to know that, Dad.

Beat.

BRIAN: Why don't you look for another job, if it's not making you happy.

ELLEN: It's not the job.

BRIAN: You were always brilliant at anything you chose to put your mind to.

ELLEN: When I was a kid.

Beat.

BRIAN: You're still young. You could do anything.

You're not *old*, are you?

ELLEN: I feel it.

Here, in this city.

I feel old and… pale, and female, and straight and single.

And I'm not Irish, and I don't surf. I'm in a minority.

They have underground bars here for people like me, they're at airports. Nobody goes to them, not even people like me. We wouldn't be seen dead in them.

Beat.

BRIAN: You just need to get out more, meet more people.

ELLEN: I've met all the people I want to here.

BRIAN: That's / not

ELLEN: I can't even bear the way people… walk in this city. Everyone's so… pleased with themselves. Whole city is, pleased with itself, with how it looks, its views, its smug fucking water views. And I'm amazed anybody here manages to make it into work at all, the amount of time they must take getting ready.

BRIAN: [*with a laugh*] Els

ELLEN: Everything here is so *fucking* shiny, hurts my eyes, to look at it. And I don't like frappés.

I hate frappés. And suntans, spray tans, sushi, swimming in ocean pools, jogging, bridges, paninis, Pilates, the harbour, sunsets, hot pants and small dogs, small gay dogs and cockroaches.

BRIAN: Nobody likes cock / roaches

ELLEN: And I'm allergic to the tap water, and then the wine seems to have stopped.

BRIAN: Stopped… what?

ELLEN: Working.

It's just not working, Dad, I don't know the rules.

BRIAN: What do you / mean?

ELLEN: This city has rules. And if you can't work them out then you're lost, afloat. Because it's hard and fast and shiny here, and it's lonely.

BRIAN: But other than that, you like the place?

ELLEN: I'm lonely, Dad.

> *Beat.*

BRIAN: I could… take you out, if you like.

I used to know some great places round here.

ELLEN: We could go to a gay bar. Though, you're not really dressed for it.

Though, you'd still probably get more attention than me.

BRIAN: I think you're being a bit dramatic.

ELLEN: No, you would get more attention than me.

> *Beat.*

BRIAN: You can't stay in here, Ellen, not forever. You need to get out, get out and, do something

ELLEN: You always stayed in, for the Series

BRIAN: For the Series, yes, but

ELLEN: I'm happy here, with you.

Aren't you, happy here?

> *Beat.*

BRIAN: It's not

ELLEN: We never did make it to a game, did we, not together.

> *Beat.*

You were going to take me with you, 2003, remember?

BRIAN: Now that, was a Series to remember.

ELLEN: Except we didn't go. You didn't end up taking me.

> *Beat.*

We could go to the Fifth Test, in Sydney, we could go to that together. I can pull some strings at work.

BRIAN: / Ellen

ELLEN: I'll bring the sunscreen and I'll let you make the sandwiches. It's a once-in-a-lifetime opportunity, to see the Fifth Test, the final one, here at the SCG.

BRIAN: I know, kiddo.

ELLEN: Please take me with you, Dad.

> *She closes her eyes.*

BRIAN: You used to do that when you were little.

> *She opens her eyes.*

Your first day at kindy, or… at school. When you didn't want to go to the doctor's.

> *She laughs.*

You'd close your eyes, tight, and pretend you were somewhere else. And you'd refuse to open them, until we promised you that it was going to be alright. Which seemed to work. Because eventually you'd open them, and whatever it was that you were afraid of seemed to have passed.

And everyone said, that child of yours, that Ellen, she has got a vivid imagination.

ELLEN: What's wrong with that?

BRIAN: Nothing. There's nothing wrong / with

ELLEN: Why can't we go, Dad?

BRIAN: You know we can't, Ellen.

Beat.

ELLEN: I thought you wanted me to care about it. But I see now you want it all to yourself.

BRIAN: Sometimes you are the spit of your mother.

ELLEN: No, Dad, I'm like you. Everybody says I'm more like you.

She looks away and then back at him.

What do you do? Where do you go?

When you leave at night, where do you go?

BRIAN: I could ask you the same thing.

I wander the streets, see if it's changed. And it has. But then everything seems to have

ELLEN: What are you looking for?

BRIAN: Probably much the same as you, Ellen.

Signs of, life.

She looks away. A moment.

I went down to see your mother.

She looks back at him.

I know it's probably the last thing she needs now. But I... I miss her, Ellen, God, I... I can't even remember what she smells like.

Somebody has pruned the jacaranda, out the front. Dead leaves all over the ground. Why would anybody, leave them like that, not, sweep them up?

We planted that tree down there when you were born, planted a seed with our own hands, to remind us, of here, of our time here in Sydney. Got more beautiful every year, these beautiful purple-blue flowers, two months of every year, that was all, but it was worth the wait. We weren't even sure if it would survive down there, but it, it flourished. You used to collect up the leaves, put them in water, in jars, say it was perfume. Made us pay a dollar for it.

He laughs.

ELLEN: Dad

BRIAN: You shouldn't prune jacarandas, everybody knows that. Probably won't even flower this year now.

Beat.

She's repainted the front of the house.

ELLEN: She… got someone in.

BRIAN: Couldn't she have waited?

ELLEN: For what, Dad?

Beat.

BRIAN: They've done a terrible fucking job. Cowboys obviously, where did she get them?

ELLEN: Somebody recommended them.

BRIAN: Who?

Maureen?

ELLEN: I'm not

BRIAN: Bet it bloody was.

She wasn't there anyway. Place was all locked up.

ELLEN: She's gone away, to the Gold Coast. Two weeks.

Beat.

BRIAN: With, Maureen?

Beat.

ELLEN: She needed a break.

BRIAN: What her, or Maureen?

Because Maureen's whole life is a break. The woman vacillates between short breaks, city breaks, mini-breaks and the occasional break, from having a break, which she then has to break, with a break.

ELLEN: You never liked Maureen.

BRIAN: It's not that I don't like her, it's not…

Your mum would never go to the Gold Coast with me, you know

ELLEN: You wouldn't get a new tent.

BRIAN: There was nothing wrong with our old tent. A tent, is for sleeping. And I was frightened if it slept more than two, Maureen was going to invite herself along.

ELLEN: She's taken your voice off the answer machine.

Beat.

I rung up, few weeks ago, expecting you, your... voice, it was always, your voice.

She hasn't recorded a new message, she's just left it, nothing, it just, rings out.

Mum says it wore out, the tape. Just stopped one day.

I didn't believe her.

BRIAN: She's never been much of a liar, your mum.

ELLEN: At first, she wanted to talk about you all the time. And then she, she stopped. Now it's like she can't even bear the sound of your name, not out loud.

Now all she wants to talk about is her new life. Its new hobbies, holiday destinations. She's brimming with it, her new fucking life.

BRIAN: Life, without Brian.

Beat.

ELLEN: Maureen was the only one there for her when you left.

Mum said everybody else acted like she was a child, a fucking child, in her sixties

BRIAN: Ellen, I didn't

ELLEN: 'Course Mum didn't say 'fucking', I just added that

BRIAN: / Els

ELLEN: For dramatic effect.

BRIAN: Listen / to me

ELLEN: She said it was like she could see herself, in everyone else's eyes. See that being alone, suddenly, made her a burden. Like they could smell it.

BRIAN: I didn't leave, Ellen.

ELLEN: Her need.

BRIAN: I died.

Beat.

I died.

My heart stopped, Ellen. It stopped beating, for too long, kiddo. And I

ELLEN: Don't

BRIAN: I died, Els.

He moves to touch her.

ELLEN: I said *don't* fucking call me that.

Beat.

BRIAN: Sorry.

Ellen.

Beat.

Old habits die hard. Never bloody break that one now.

He laughs, quietly, and then looks tremendously sad.

I took a couple of breaths. I remember that, one normal and then one slightly bigger

But something wasn't right. Because by then my brain was trying its best to pump blood through my lungs, pump it, for dear life, throughout the rest of my body. I felt a bit dizzy, nothing to write home about. They say you feel pain, you're supposed to. Left arm for some reason, and then your chest, like a weight. That's what they say. But I didn't. I didn't even really know it was happening, until

Which is probably something. No time to really think about it, to know what's coming next. Because that, that would be a terrifying thought.

No, all I thought, I remember thinking this as I opened the fridge, to get some cool water. Best thing I ever bought, that fridge with the chiller. It was a stinking night, hadn't cooled down, not even at two a.m., air like, soup. Your mother was dead to the world, snoring, like an angel.

I opened the fridge and I thought, hang on a minute, what's that, that feeling. Because, I've given up smoking. I've given up full-fat cheese. I even said I'll sign up for the that yoga at the funny church your mum likes, that's if Maureen doesn't fucking come, in her onesie and I've just bought my first three-man tent, for when the rain stops, so what's this? What, is, this?

Beat.

There was another breath then, in between that thought, that moment and the next one. The next thought, I thought I was going to have. And

God, I wanted one, a breath. I wanted to fill up my lungs, breathe it in, air. Life. So much.

Life.

By then my brain had been deprived of oxygen for too long. It was probably only ten or twenty seconds, at the most, but that's too long. The brain starts to die then, and that's when you cease to breathe, and then, well it's over then. And you. You die.

Beat.

I died, Ellen.

She stares ahead, refusing to look at him, crying silently. He reaches out to touch her and then remembers that he cannot. They sit in silence for a moment.

The lights fade.

SCENE SEVEN

In the darkness, we hear select moments from the radio coverage of the Fourth Test. If there has been an interval, it can be heard as the audience are coming back in.

Crucially, we hear the moment at which it starts to become obvious that Australia are going to lose and we hear its dramatic final moments play out.

Then silence.

A knock at the door.

The sound of a radio, loud, but playing nothing in particular—late-night radio, perhaps a chat/help line.

Lights come up. ELLEN *is on the floor and the cricket is long over. She looks like a broken doll, hair and make-up awry. She holds the cricket bat in one hand, a bottle of nearly-drunk champagne in the other.*

The apartment looks like it has been hit by a hurricane, everything that can be upturned, has been. The suitcase, still closed, is on the floor in the middle of the room. Another knock.

ELLEN *reacts as if only now hearing it for the first time. She gets up, cricket bat in hand, and unsteadily walks to the door, as if it might be salvation.*

She opens it. ADAM *is standing there, about to knock again.*
A moment.

ADAM: [*loud, to be heard over the radio*] Thought maybe you weren't in.

ELLEN: I thought you were somebody else.

ADAM: Yeah, I've had that before.

Then I heard your radio.

Think the whole floor can probably hear your radio. Possibly all of Potts Point. Elizabeth Bay. Didn't even know they could go that loud.

I tried your bell for a bit.

ELLEN: Doesn't work.

ADAM: No, I realise that now. Then if it did, work, you probably wouldn't have been able to hear it, over the

> *She turns her back on him, finds the radio amongst the chaos, and turns it off.*

ELLEN: What are you doing here?

ADAM: Adam

> *In case she's forgotten:*

I'm… / Adam

ELLEN: What are you doing here, Adam?

ADAM: Sorry, I've still got this ringing in my ears.

Mind if I…

> *She doesn't move. He comes into the apartment and looks around at the state of it.*

You moving?

ELLEN: No.

ADAM: Your place, it looks like you've re-arranged.

> *Beat.*

ELLEN: There was a cockroach.

ADAM: Just the one?

> *She turns and looks at him.*

You've got something in your eye.

> *She puts a hand up to her face.*

You've got quite a lot of, there's quite a lot of stuff all over your face actually.

She turns away from him to wipe her face and then turns back.

ELLEN: I wasn't expecting guests.

ADAM: Thought you were.

You said… you thought I was somebody / else

ELLEN: Look, it's not a good time right now, Adam.

ADAM: [*nodding*] For what?

ELLEN: I'm not in the mood for… for company.

ADAM: No. I wasn't really planning on coming round.

Couldn't believe I even remembered where you lived. Though I'm starting to realise I've got a pretty good memory. Compared to most, well compared to

ELLEN: Me?

ADAM: Yeah.

Beat.

I heard about the cricket. It's not going so

ELLEN: We lost

Beat.

ADAM: Yeah, but. Only the Fourth Test. It's still only / the

ELLEN: You were right, we were slammed, killed, we've lost and it's over.

Beat.

ADAM: I'm sorry.

ELLEN: Why? You don't even like cricket.

ADAM: It's not that I don't.

No, I don't really.

But I could

ELLEN: What are you doing here, Adam? What do you want?

Beat.

ADAM: It's Christmas

ELLEN: Christmas is over too.

ADAM: It's still the season of goodwill, good

ELLEN: Thank fuck.

ADAM: … cheer.

Beat.

ELLEN: I hate Christmas. I hate everything about this time of year.

I find it's easier not to go out. That way, you can avoid carol singers and Secret Santa, having to buy people cards with pictures of fucking snow on, when it's forty degrees outside, and I don't have to buy a load of cheap shiny shit for people I can't even pretend to like for the rest of the year.

He holds out a very badly wrapped present.

ADAM: Happy Christmas.

Beat.

ELLEN: Why would you

ADAM: I wanted to.

He holds out the present again.

It really isn't anything

He holds it there until she takes it.

You don't have to open it now

She puts it on the pouffe and walks away from it.

You can open it later

He looks disappointed.

ELLEN: What do you want, Adam?

ADAM: I wanted to see if you were alright.

ELLEN: Why? Why do you want to be my friend?

ADAM: I don't want to be your friend.

Beat.

ELLEN: And, I don't want company.

Beat.

ADAM: It's just that last time, we didn't end on a very good note

ELLEN: So, why repeat it?

Beat.

I'm fine. Really.

She tries to usher him towards the door.

I'm fine, Adam.

ADAM: You don't look fine.

ELLEN: Yeah, well like I said, nothing is what it looks like round here.

ADAM: [*impersonating Jack Lemmon in* The Apartment] And nobody should be alone on New Year's Eve.

Beat.

You are aware it's New Year's Eve tonight, right?

She looks at him. He's unsure whether this is a 'yes', or a 'no'.

And I hate New Year's Eve.

Probably as much as you hate Christmas.

As he speaks, he starts to slowly pick things up, one by one, that are upturned.

Hammy, my first hamster, my only hamster as it turned out, died on New Year's Eve.

I was so scarred by it, they thought it was better if I didn't get another one.

It was my fault.

ELLEN: Adam

ADAM: No it was, it was my fault. I gave him, Hammy, an extra serving of food, what with it being, well everybody else seemed to be over-indulging and I thought he deserved to mark the occasion too, and not just with another spin on his wheel, I mean life had to be more than that, even for Hammy.

Turns out hamsters shouldn't, over-indulge. Not for a special occasion. Not even, once a year.

Beat.

I was only eight, but it was, you know, bit of a turning point.

I learned that night that New Year's Eve is the one night of the year where, whatever it is you think is going to happen, don't, don't think it. Because the only thing you can bank on, on New Year's Eve, is it being the biggest let-down, of your life.

Beat.

So, I thought maybe you'd like to do something.

ELLEN: Why?

ADAM: I thought we could both get rid of any expectations of anything remotely eventful, successful, happening, and just, go with it.

Beat.

ELLEN: I'm

I don't want to do anything

ADAM: Yeah, but you see, that's the whole point. The whole point is to avoid, parties, crowds, festivities. People even.

ELLEN: Then why bother going out at all

ADAM: Because I think you probably need to.

ELLEN: You don't know me.

ADAM: And because, it's starting to smell in here a bit.

Beat.

ELLEN: I don't want to go out, Adam. I want to stay here. I don't want to go out and I *can't*. I'm sorry.

He nods.

ADAM: At least open your present.

Realising he's not going to go, she goes over and picks up the present.

Wrapping's not really my

Inside the paper is a single woman's high-heeled shoe. She holds it up.

ELLEN: It's a… a shoe

ADAM: Yeah, I know.

I was going to buy you a lamp, but then I thought, well you'd probably break it.

It's yours

She looks at him.

ELLEN: What?

ADAM: You left it at my place, the shoe.

She looks at the shoe—as if it almost brings something back, but not quite.

ELLEN: When?

ADAM: The first night, we met.

ELLEN: When? How long ago, Adam?

ADAM: Two years.

Beat.

It was two years ago.

ELLEN: You've... kept this, held onto it, for two

ADAM: I thought one day you might want it.

She holds it close to her.

ELLEN: Thank you

ADAM: You say that a lot

No, hang on, you never say that. I've never heard you say that before.

Beat.

ELLEN: Thank you.

A moment. They look at each other.

I'm sorry I don't remember it. The night we met.

ADAM: Which one of them?

ELLEN: It's not personal.

ADAM: Kind of is, actually.

Beat.

ELLEN: I don't make a habit of...

ADAM: Remembering?

ELLEN: Getting things back.

Things I've lost.

I've lost a lot of things.

They never come back.

ADAM: They're just, things.

Beat.

ELLEN: Thank you, for the shoe, and for

Beat.

I'd like to be alone now.

Beat.

ADAM: Right. With your shoe.

Beat.

ELLEN: Yes.

ADAM: Right.

I'll

He slowly starts to head for the door.

ELLEN: What are you going to do?

Tonight?

Beat.

ADAM: I was thinking of trying to avoid the crowds.

She nods. A beat.

ELLEN: How are you going to do that?

ADAM: I have this theory. That everyone's pretty much going to head towards the one spot, because, well because it's tonight, and because, well because most people lack imagination.

So I'm thinking, if I avoid that spot, I might get lucky. Carve out a niche

She nods.

I'm thinking of… maybe buying a bottle of chardonnay and finding a quiet

ELLEN: I don't like chardonnay.

Beat.

ADAM: Right. You… don't

ELLEN: No.

Beat.

ADAM: Right. What about… a pinot?

She shakes her head.

Sauvignon blanc?

ELLEN: If it's from New Zealand

ADAM: Not very patriotic.

ELLEN: I like the Marlborough ones the best.

Beat.

ADAM: Right.

Beat.

So, so I've got this chilled bottle of Marlborough's finest sauvignon blanc. And I head down towards the harbour

ELLEN: Why would you… I mean everyone's there

ADAM: Yeah, but I've got this special route.

You see, I get away from The Cross and go pretty much down to the end of Macleay.

You can go behind the college on Challis, but I prefer to take a left at St Neot and cut through to the steps, the McElhone steps, at the bottom of which you're on Wylde. Then you sidestep Garden Island to cross Cowper Wharf which brings you to Lincoln Corner, managing to pretty much avoid the Eastern Distributor. Nobody else would be stupid enough to go that way, it's the longest way round and involves the most steps.

She laughs, quietly.

Then I follow that all the way round, edge of the water. Through Woolloomooloo, bypass the Domain, the art gallery. Then cut through the Botanic Gardens. 'Course they'd be locked, but you can slip in, I slip in, just by the State Library, there's a low bit in the wall there, you can climb over. And then it's past Palm House, through where the black mondo grass and the fire plants are, through the Northern Depot Gate, over the bridge that leads you onto Cahill Walk and straight through to Macquarie, which you follow all the way down until you hit the Quay.

And then I'm there.

ELLEN: Are you?

ADAM: Yeah, that's my shortcut.

And of course everyone's distracted, because there's this guy, doing this, well it's not really a show, but he's got this didgeridoo, it's for the tourists, he's not even indigenous, so he shouldn't really be playing one. It's an insult really

ELLEN: But, if it's for tourists

ADAM: Yeah. And he's actually quite good. So anyway, everyone's… all crowded round him, so I just duck down the back, behind them, duck down to Wharf Five and get a ticket.

There isn't even a queue, because everyone's

ELLEN: For what?

ADAM: For the ferry.

> *Beat.*

ELLEN: The ferry?

ADAM: Yeah.

ELLEN: To… where?

ADAM: Take your pick

Neutral Bay, Mosman, Watson's. Balmain, which is my personal pick. Kissing Point.

ELLEN: But it's New Year's Eve.

ADAM: And, what people don't realise is, there is a ferry that runs from the Quay on New Year's Eve, it just keeps itself quiet. The last one goes at eight forty-five.

To Balmain.

ELLEN: How do you

ADAM: So, which one is it going to be? Which ferry should it be?

> *Beat.*

ELLEN: Balmain.

ADAM: You… sure?

ELLEN: [*nodding*] I've never been to Balmain.

ADAM: Really? You don't know what you're missing.

So, I'm on the ferry. Didn't even end up getting a ticket, but they let me on. And the ferry pulls out, and it's hot, stinking in the city and packed. But on the ferry, there's this beautiful breeze, sea breeze. It's the perfect temperature.

Can you feel it?

The breeze. Through your hair, on the back of your neck.

She closes her eyes.

It's perfect.

She opens them.

And you can see the whole city. Luna Park, look there's people swimming in the pool, some of them have got their clothes on. There's Milson's Point.

There's the Sydney Opera House.

ELLEN: With its tiles.

ADAM: And of course the fireworks have started up by now. You can see them from the boat, it's a really good view

She's looking at him.

What?

ELLEN: I don't like fireworks. They frighten me. A bit.

ADAM: It's just the children's fireworks at this point.

She's not convinced.

But you know what, I don't like the fact that you can pay in this city, to go somewhere and get a better view of them. Because nobody should have to pay for fireworks.

ELLEN: No.

ADAM: Fuck the fireworks. Come on.

He holds out his hand.

They're almost behind us now, they've almost run out of bang and they're behind us now, just lighting up the sky, but it's fading.

He's holding out his hand. She looks at it, but she doesn't take it.

And we're there now. We're at Balmain. They're behind us.

We're at Darling Street. There's this little old building, run-down sandstone thing, looks like a church. And we're going in.

ELLEN: Are we?

ADAM: To the building.

ELLEN: Why? You said it was derelict, it might be

ADAM: I've hidden two champagne glasses in there, in a tea towel under a rock.

ELLEN: But

But we're drinking a Marlborough sauvignon blanc.

ADAM: Only because you wanted to. You chose it, the wine

She smiles.

We can go and get some champagne, if / you

ELLEN: No it's fine. I mean, I'm happy with this.

ADAM: Right.

So, we go in, it's dark, but we can just make out inside, because of the moon, and the glasses are still there, still behind the rock under the tea towel, I knew they would be, and we get them out and we cross over Darling Street

ELLEN: Where are we going now?

ADAM: Hold your horses, we've come this far, we're nearly there. Come on

She takes his hand, as if without realising it.

And. Here we are.

ELLEN: Where?

ADAM: The park. Thornton Park, on the water. Best spot in, best view of the city anywhere in Sydney. And there's this tree, this big beautiful old tree. And we sit under it, it's almost dark now

ELLEN: Almost?

No, I mean, if we got the ferry a while ago. Wouldn't it be

ADAM: It's dark.

Though the fireworks, they've left this kind of light, in the sky. And you open the wine. You do the honours, as you chose it, and we pour ourselves a glass and it's still chilled

ELLEN: Are there people there?

ADAM: Hardly anyone

ELLEN: Really?

ADAM: Everyone's in the city. They think that's where they should be, they're at a party, they've paid to go somewhere where they think they're going to get this perfect view, when actually

ELLEN: We've got it.

Beat.

ADAM: And we sit on the grass and there's still a breeze and we drink our wine and watch the city, it's there for us.

And it's beautiful.

They're still holding hands. They look.

See.

ELLEN: [*quietly*] Yes.

Pause.

I'm a bit hungry.

I haven't eaten for

ADAM: We could go and

ELLEN: No, I don't want to go anywhere else.

ADAM: Okay.

ELLEN: Can we just stay here?

ADAM: Okay.

Beat. He stands up, holds out a hand to her.

ELLEN: What?

ADAM: Dance with me

ELLEN: To… what?

ADAM: Use your imagination.

Beat.

ELLEN: I can't.

ADAM: Yes you can.

She takes his hand and stands up. They move closer, but don't move.

ELLEN: I can't

They are close now, though not moving.

ADAM: It's nice

Your… smell

She breaks away.

No, I, I like / it.

Beat.

ELLEN: What is it? What do I… smell of?

She looks afraid. He leans in closer, smells her.

ADAM: It's.

It's like… I think it's… jacaranda.

She stays standing, very still. A pause, longer than a beat.

ELLEN: Something happened to me.

Beat.

Something, terrible, happened.

Beat.

Two years ago

And I

I'm still

I lost… something, important.

Beat.

It's not coming back.

ADAM: It's okay.

ELLEN: It isn't.

ADAM: / Ellen

ELLEN: It isn't okay.

Beat.

ADAM: No

I think I knew that.

I mean, I think I understand.

Because

Beat.

Well, Hammy.

ELLEN: It's not really the same

ADAM: No, but

I just mean

ELLEN: It isn't.

Pause.

I could stay like this for a while.

If we had more wine.

ADAM: Unless it rains

He looks at her. She's still holding his hand.

ELLEN: I don't mind. I like it, the rain.

They move closer.

We hear something signalling midnight outside.

ADAM: And then, after a while, after some time, somewhere the clocks strike twelve. But we don't notice

ELLEN: Happy New Year

Beat.

ADAM: I have to say, that is the best New Year's Eve, I've ever had. By far. And the cheapest. And you know possibly the

ELLEN: Stop.

Just, stop.

Beat.

Stop talking.

She leans forward and kisses him on the mouth. He lets her.

The lights fade as they continue kissing.

SCENE EIGHT

Lights up on Ellen's apartment. The place has been tidied, everything is now off the floor and the bed is made. The suitcase now rests up against the wall, by the door. There is no sign of cricket paraphernalia.

BRIAN sits on the end of the bed, waiting, as if he's been waiting a while. He is dressed, though his feet are bare.

ELLEN lets herself in. She enters and drops her keys in a bowl, before seeing BRIAN. ELLEN is now tidier too. She wears a dress and is glowing, damp from the rain—something about her lighter. She carries a shopping bag.

BRIAN: Don't tell me you've been in to work.

She stops, turns to look at him. She doesn't smile. A beat.

ELLEN: No.

> *She turns away from him.*

Office is closed.

BRIAN: Well, was only a matter of time. I'm amazed the place stayed running as long as it did, what with half the staff never there.

ELLEN: It's the third of January. Most places are closed

BRIAN: Not the massage parlour downstairs.

> Still, people will always need. Well, massage.

ELLEN: I didn't expect you to be here.

> *Beat.*

BRIAN: You know what I'm like, Ellen, with… dates, with. Time.

> Of course, it's worse now. Now I've got all eternity to lose track of

> *She starts to take off her wet shoes.*

Still raining?

I'd forgotten how it comes down at this time of the year, sweltering one moment and then the next, everyone's running for cover, drenched. Not sure how I forgot that.

I got stuck out in it as well.

> *Beat.*

ELLEN: Did you?

BRIAN: I stood right out in it. Right in the middle of the road, arms outstretched. But I didn't feel a thing. I could see it hit the road, run over the road, where my feet should be, for some reason that upset me a bit. Always upsets me, that bit.

Stupid fucking thing to miss, rain, feeling rain, but it is one of the things I miss most.

> *Beat.*

ELLEN: I thought you weren't coming back.

BRIAN: What?

And miss the last Test?

ELLEN: You weren't here, for the last one.

I waited for you.

BRIAN: Yes, well half the Australian team wasn't there, not really, not awake and present for the Fourth Test. Let's face it.

Beat.

ELLEN: You... watched it... somewhere else?

She is angry.

[*Looking up*] Shit... you managed to get satellite put in, up there? What did they get, Sky fucking TV. For your sins?

She laughs.

BRIAN: You're upset, I can see that.

ELLEN: Yes.

BRIAN: That isn't why I came, to upset you.

ELLEN: Then why did you come, Dad? What are you here for?

He looks at her. A long beat.

BRIAN: In 1882, after Australia beat England, *The Times* ran a mock obituary.

It read, 'In affectionate remembrance of English cricket which died at The Oval today. RIP. The body will be cremated...

ELLEN: ... and the ashes taken to Australia.'

Beat.

BRIAN: That was when the English still had a sense of humour.

ELLEN: I thought you'd come back for me.

I believed that and it made me so... happy.

BRIAN: I said I was sorry, and I'm here now, aren't I?

ELLEN: And it's over, Dad, it's over.

She glares at him.

BRIAN: I came back to see you, Ellen.

Alright, I admit it was a bit of a bonus, to be here when the Series was on, but that's not why I

I mean, do you think this is fun for me?

ELLEN: What?

BRIAN: Come on, you've got to admit there's a certain... cruel irony to it.

I die, the night before the last Test, two years ago, couldn't even hang

on long enough to see us fucking triumph. And then I'm brought back
from the fucking dead and forced to watch us lose.

ELLEN: On my birthday

BRIAN: What?

ELLEN: You died the night of my birthday, do you remember that?

> *Beat.*

BRIAN: Yes, yes of course I

ELLEN: You didn't always remember it.

BRIAN: I didn't always forget.

> *Beat.*

ELLEN: Nobody forced you to come back.

BRIAN: And if I'd known it was going to end like this, I wouldn't have
bloody bothered.

> *He looks at her, wanting to take that back—but it's too late.*

ELLEN: Do you like spending time with me, Dad?

BRIAN: What?

ELLEN: Do you like me, Dad?

Do you like me at all?

> *Beat.*

BRIAN: How can you ask me that?

Ellen. You're my daughter

ELLEN: / Yes.

BRIAN: Why do you have to make everything so, emotional?

ELLEN: Because, that's me, I'm emotional

BRIAN: But why can't you just… try / and

ELLEN: Don't tell me to *fucking relax*.

> *Beat.*

BRIAN: You used to be so happy.

You were this, bright, funny, beautiful girl. So… happy, and clever,
alive. Everyone wanted to be around you, you had so many… lovely
friends. Everyone wanted to be near you.

ELLEN: What do you think happened, Dad?

What do you think?

Beat.

BRIAN: I'm here, Ellen.

   I am

ELLEN: And every time you leave, it's like, like I'm losing you all over
   again.

   Beat.

BRIAN: I'm sorry

   I'm so

   So

   Sorry.

   Beat.

ELLEN: You say that a lot.

   Beat.

   Did you always, did you always say it a lot?

BRIAN: Can't remember. Probably.

   Not enough, probably.

   Beat.

   Ellen, you are my daughter.

   And you are. To me. You're, the Don.

ELLEN: What?

BRIAN: Donald Bradman.

   Ellen. You. You're the best person I've ever met.

   She is crying.

ELLEN: Then why did you die?

   How is that… fair?

   Who made that… fucking rule?

BRIAN: There are no rules, Ellen. Life doesn't work like that

ELLEN: What about death?

BRIAN: No, no rules there either, kiddo.

   Beat.

   I wish I could hold you.

He walks to her, close, almost touching, stops. He looks at her.

You know it's not, up there. Where I go, isn't up, at all

Everybody thinks that, refers to it, as being up. Anyway, turns out it isn't.

It's on the side. Those of us that have died, we go... over there. To this place... in the periphery, the, wings. Just out of reach.

She looks at him.

ELLEN: What do you do there?

BRIAN: I hang about mostly, I mooch.

He laughs to himself.

And I dream.

I dream of my life. I miss, my life.

But I know it's a dream, because I know it's over. That I had a life, that was worth missing.

ELLEN: A good innings.

He smiles.

I met someone

BRIAN: I know.

She looks at him.

ELLEN: How do you

BRIAN: I know that he's different from the others.

Then the others all looked the same to me.

ELLEN: He doesn't follow the cricket

BRIAN: In truth, Ellen, neither do you.

ELLEN: He said he wants me to explain it to him.

BRIAN: Thank fuck I'm dead.

Though at least we know he's not a father substitute.

She smiles.

ELLEN: We've only just met and, I'm not

I'm not sure

BRIAN: Of what?

ELLEN: I'm not sure of anything.

BRIAN: You just need to

ELLEN: I know.

He walks over to the suitcase, looks at it.

I lost your watch.

Your favourite one

BRIAN: Not the one with the leather / strap

ELLEN: I'm sorry, Dad

BRIAN: It's alright, Ellen.

It doesn't matter. It's just a watch.

Just things, Els.

ELLEN: Your things. They're all I've got left.

BRIAN: That's not true.

He smiles at her. He looks at the suitcase and then back at her.

But how could you let them play that song?

ELLEN: What?

BRIAN: I mean, Sandy bloody Denny, Ellen, at my funeral.

ELLEN: It was Fairport Convention.

BRIAN: What about… something by Elvis Costello, 'Accidents Will Happen', or or… 'I Don't Want to Go to Chelsea'? Or the Stones, what about, 'Not Fade Away' by the

ELLEN: Mum loved that song.

She loves it.

And I chose it, for her.

Beat.

Guess you had to be there, Dad.

He nods. Then he looks back at the suitcase.

BRIAN: Two years.

Two bloody years

ELLEN: It's two years since I moved into this flat.

BRIAN: Still haven't unpacked.

She looks at the suitcase.

ELLEN: I moved in here, the day you…

BRIAN: I know.

Beat.

ELLEN: I should have been there.

BRIAN: You were getting on with your life.

ELLEN: Mum called me.

She kept calling

That night… the night you. I turned the phone off.

BRIAN: You didn't know.

Beat.

I couldn't put a foot wrong, could I, kiddo, not in your eyes. Thank you for that.

Beat.

Call her, Ellen. Call your mum.

ELLEN: You don't know what it's like now, Dad, without you around

BRIAN: Yes I do.

Beat.

She's back, from the Gold Coast.

He smiles.

I stood in the window, our window, willing her to turn round, and when she did, she couldn't see me.

ELLEN: She's moved on.

This hurts him, and then both.

BRIAN: Has she?

ELLEN: She's moving on.

Beat.

BRIAN: What if she's doing that for you?

ELLEN: I missed it, Dad.

I wasn't there

BRIAN: It was over in a minute, kiddo, and I was gone then.

ELLEN: But I

BRIAN: I was gone.

Pause.

You've made a life for yourself here now.

Beat.

You will.

ELLEN: This isn't a city for...

BRIAN: For what?

ELLEN: Grieving.

BRIAN: No, it's a city for living. And that's what you're doing, Ellen, you're living. You are.

Beat.

ELLEN: Adam's coming over.

We're going to listen to it, to the last day, on the radio.

I told him that, even though it was over, even though England retains the Ashes now, whatever happens.

BRIAN *looks pained.*

I told him that if we take it to the fifth day, then it's still something.

BRIAN: That's my girl.

ELLEN: And then he's going to take me out, show me the city, his city.

BRIAN: For your birthday?

ELLEN: Yes.

BRIAN: [*looking at his watch*] Well, play starts... any minute.

Beat.

ELLEN: He'll be here soon.

He nods.

BRIAN: This morning they said that as Australia desperately tried to... prepare, regroup, for the Fifth Test, there was an aura of calmness surrounding the English camp. And of course, they've earned that, to be fair.

The thing about a five-Test Series, is it does sort out the better team. And England, were that, this time. Even though half of them are South African.

In a true Ashes battle, the separation lies, in one side doing what the other couldn't.

Beat.

ELLEN: I should get ready, Dad.

BRIAN: [*nodding*] I feel like Ricky Ponting.

She looks at him.

I know it's time to go.

He doesn't move. He looks at her.

There's something, for your birthday. It's in the bag.

She looks over to the suitcase.

Call her.

Your mum.

You've got your whole life ahead of you.

He goes to the door. Beat.

ELLEN: Dad

BRIAN: Close your eyes

Beat.

Close your eyes, kiddo.

She closes them, he leaves, She waits a moment and then opens them. He's gone.

She gets up. She lays the suitcase flat on the floor. She breathes.

She opens the suitcase and takes out a beautifully wrapped present. She opens it—it is an old worn cricket ball. She smells it. It smells of her dad.

She then takes out a pair of worn brogues, a pair of faded Levis, a worn leather jacket, a comb, a book and an old leather wallet. She takes them out one by one, lays them on the bed. She then takes out his ashes, in a box, something that looks precious.

She gets up and goes to the window and opens the blind. The morning light fills the room and there's a city view—a beautiful view. Her eyes adjust to the light, as it falls on her.

There is a knock at the door. She stands there in the light for a moment, before placing the ashes somewhere where they are visible. She moves towards the door to open it, as the lights fade.

SCENE NINE

We hear a door burst open. ADAM *bursts into the room first.*
Lights up on Adam's flat, a bare, neat flat with hardly anything in it.
ELLEN *then follows. She is a little drunk and she's laughing, full of beans.*

ADAM: Your turn.

> *She laughs again.*

[*Laughing*] What?

ELLEN: You. You and your

> Key. Under… the mat

> *She laughs, staggers a little, straightens up. She looks at him. He looks at her.*

This isn't Canada.

ADAM: What?

> *She laughs.*

And it's still your turn.

> *She looks around the flat.*

ELLEN: Hey, I just moved too.

> *He looks at her—unsure what she means.*

I've just moved into my apartment too. Today. From today on, this, is my new city, my new life.

ADAM: I've… I've been here, in this apartment for a while.

ELLEN: Really?

ADAM: I just… don't have a lot of stuff yet. Not even sure if I'm going to stay.

Haven't decided.

ELLEN: Could you get us that drink, while you're thinking about it? You said you'd make us both a drink.

ADAM: Yeah, well you said you'd dance with me. That you'd show me how to dance.

ELLEN: And you said you lived in a nice place.

ADAM: No, no I said if you came back, to my place, it'd be nice.

She grins.

It's still your turn.

He goes to her, holds his arm out, to take her bag. She giggles, the bag seems to have wrapped itself around her. She tries to unravel it, unsuccessfully.

Here.

He gently unravels the bag and peels it off her, something tender in it.

[*Feeling its weight*] Shit, what have you got in here?

ELLEN: Most of my new life.

She grins.

ADAM: Now it's my turn.

He takes his top off, to reveal his chest. She looks away, then looks back.

Your turn again.

He is looking at her. Beat. She takes a shoe off.

Hey, those aren't the rules.

She laughs.

But, when you laugh like that, you know I don't mind you breaking a few, rules.

She goes to his window, looks out.

ELLEN: Mine's better than yours.

ADAM: What?

ELLEN: My view.

But still

She looks out, at the world.

That is…

ADAM: What?

ELLEN: Takes your breath away.

All that… life.

ADAM: You make me feel
   Like anything is possible.

ELLEN: Where are we again?

ADAM: Balmain

ELLEN: [*turning back to him*] And, is getting a fucking drink in Balmain
   possible?

   He smiles.

   It's my birthday, and right now I'd like a drink.

   Beat.

ADAM: Is it, is it really your birthday?

   She leans down and pulls off her other shoe.

   Why didn't you tell me?

ELLEN: It's just a day.

   Like any other, nothing special about it.

   *She flings the shoe hard across the room, it disappears. She holds
   up her arms.*

   Six!

   Your turn.

   She grins at him.

ADAM: Why were you out on your own, on your birthday?

ELLEN: Don't know anyone here yet.

ADAM: You do now.

ELLEN: And because for one night I can be anyone I want here, do anything I want. Start the year how I mean to go on.

ADAM: You are really something. Whoever you are.

ELLEN: I'm Ellen

ADAM: I know.

   They look at each other. Beat.

   I'd quite like to kiss you now, Ellen.

   Beat.

ELLEN: Okay.

ADAM: Okay?

ELLEN: Yes.

ADAM: I thought… you said wanted a drink

ELLEN: Think I've probably had enough to drink, tonight.

So kiss me, quick, while it's still my birthday, while I'm still

He goes to her, cuts her off with a kiss. They kiss. He breaks away.

ADAM: Wow.

ELLEN: What?

ADAM: I'm waiting for you to get your breath back.

Beat.

Only fair.

She smiles. They kiss again. She pulls away.

ELLEN: Can you… turn the light off

He stops kissing her, takes a step back.

ADAM: Why?

Look at you. You're

I've been trying to look at you all night without you noticing, without looking like a perv, and now I can, finally look at you. So

ELLEN: I've got this rash.

ADAM: What?

ELLEN: I'm allergic to something, here, they're not sure what it is, they think maybe it's the water. And now I've got this, rash, all over me

ADAM: Wow

ELLEN: It's not catching or

ADAM: Ellen, it's alright.

ELLEN: I just, I don't want you to see it.

He touches her.

ADAM: Okay.

It's okay.

Because when I take my glasses off, I'm blind, can't see a thing. Look.

He takes his glasses off. She laughs. They start kissing again with the light on. He begins to try and take her dress off—it's a compli-cated affair.

ELLEN: Wait.

> *He stops.*

ADAM: What?

ELLEN: I think I

I need a glass of water.

> *He smiles. He exits to the kitchen.*

> *She smiles and wanders over to a record player, which sits on the floor, a pile of records stacked neatly beside it. She looks through the records, occasionally laughing quietly to herself. She picks one up, looks closely at it.*

[*Calling out*] You and my dad have the same music taste.

ADAM: [*entering with a glass of water*] Shit.

Is that shit? Or is that great?

ELLEN: My dad'd think it's great.

> *He takes the water to her. She takes it from him, takes a sip. She pulls a face.*

ADAM: What?

ELLEN: The water here, tastes like the bottom of a swimming pool. I'll never get used to that.

> *She puts the water down on the floor. She looks at him.*

ADAM: Now, where were we?

> *They start to kiss again. They begin to take her dress off when her phone begins to ring, in her bag. It rings for a while. They try to ignore it, but it gets louder.*

ELLEN: Sorry, that's, that's me.

ADAM: It's alright.

> *He breaks away.*

Though, who'd call at two in the

> *It stops ringing. They start kissing again. The phone starts ringing again.*

Do you want to

ELLEN: Sorry.

She goes over to her bag. The phone's still ringing as she's trying to find it.

ADAM: Thought you said you didn't know anyone here.

ELLEN: I don't.

She locates it.

So I'm not even going to

Without looking at it, she turns the sound off.

There.

Beat. He goes to step towards her, kicks over her glass of water.

ADAM: Shit.

Sorry.

I'll just

He goes as if about to exit.

ELLEN: Can we start again?

Can we start again, Adam?

Beat.

ADAM: Okay.

ELLEN: Who's turn is it?

ADAM: Not sure.

ELLEN: Can I, put something on?

ADAM: You're supposed to take something off.

ELLEN: A record.

I'll be gentle. Promise.

Beat.

ADAM: Be my guest.

ELLEN goes to the stereo. She chooses a record, carefully takes it out of its sleeve and puts it on the turntable. She puts the needle gently onto the record.

'I Don't Want To Go To Chelsea' by Elvis Costello begins to play. The record is old, but in mint condition. They listen a moment together. She stands up. And then somehow they move closer together, slowly and almost to the music. He is standing close to her.

ELLEN: Your turn.

They begin to dance, joyful and close.

The phone begins to ring again. We may see it, but we do not hear it.

They dance, and dance, as the lights fade.

Into blackout.

Immediately after the curtain call, 'Who Knows Where the Time Goes?', by Fairport Convention, plays. The song should play out until it is finished, including whilst the audience leaves.

THE END

GRIFFIN THEATRE COMPANY PRESENTS
THE WORLD PREMIERE OF

THIS YEAR'S ASHES
BY JANE BODIE

This Year's Ashes was co-commissioned
by Griffin Theatre Company and PlayWriting
Australia and first produced by Griffin Theatre
Company on 12 October 2011 at the SBW
Stables Theatre, Kings Cross. The play was
developed with the support of Mary Wilson
and James Emmett.

Director Shannon Murphy
Assistant Director Brandon Martignago
Designer Rita Carmody
Lighting Designer Verity Hampson
Composer Steve Francis
Sound Designer Nate Edmondson

With Belinda Bromilow, Tony
Llewellyn-Jones, Nathan Lovejoy

G T C
R H O
I E M
F A P
F T A
I R N
N E Y

holding
redlich
lawyers

playwriting
australia

Australian Government

Australia Council
for the Arts

NSW
GOVERNMENT

Communities
arts nsw

As any Australian can tell you, cricket is the unofficial soundtrack of SUMMER. Having grown up overseas, I can't claim to be as devoted as a true blue cricket fanatic. However, I understand the passion and spirit the Ashes awakens in those who are. One of the things that drew me to Jane's writing was the idea that 'Cricket, at its best, is pure theatre'. Over the past year, I have come to learn that life is just as complex as understanding the traditions of cricket and that everyone has their own perspective of any particular match up.

It is a joy and a privilege to work on a new Australian play especially one that captures Sydney in such a refreshing light. If cricket bowls me out, Sydney hits me for six! It has been a long time since a play has explored, with such detail, the intricacies of this beautiful city and the lives of those within it. I know that this play will resonate with both Sydneysiders and visitors of all generations now and in the future.

Staging modern romantic comedies has become a rarity in today's theatrical climate, possibly as a result of their immense popularity in film. Jane's natural sense of humour is so infectious in her writing that on numerous occasions it has provoked the rehearsal room to come to a halt, while tears of laughter stream down our faces!

I commend Jane for her unabashed honesty in her writing and the delicacy with which she writes about all things love, life and cricket.

Shannon Murphy

DIRECTOR'S NOTE

Firstly it's important to say that I have always wanted to write a romantic comedy, however I never imagined myself writing a play about cricket.

In 2003 I left Melbourne and moved back to London. Three years ago during the 2008 Ashes series something happened, something catastrophic and life changing. I was offered a job in Sydney a year later. At the time I couldn't foresee myself ever recovering from what had taken place, so I took the only escape route – to move far away to a new place and hope to leave the pain behind. Of course the inevitable healing process I was already in followed me. It's fair to say as part of this process I drank a lot of wine and watched a lot of rom-coms.

After I'd been living in Sydney a while, trying to carve out a life, I realised I was in the grip of a powerful grief. I then did the only thing I know to do when consumed by something, I began to think about how I might write about it, about the language and form I might use to tell its story.

I began to think about the romantic comedy. Whilst I have always loved this genre, it struck me that in recent years it seemed to have become tired and somehow out of date. Rather than being because we no longer want to laugh or see stories about love, surely this has more to do with our contemporary notions of relationships, sexuality and intimacy – we now need new ways of telling love stories, new ways of believing in love and how it might be found. I read millions of supposed rules on how to write a rom-com, the only one that struck any chord was 'Always remember romantic means sexy and comedy means funny'. I then thought about the fact that I am someone that hates rules and following them. But I couldn't help thinking about the fact that in both the loss of a loved one, and the loss of love, it is as if all the rules we believed existed have been violently broken. The world feels suddenly lawless, as if justice and balance will never be restored. Then many believe there are five stages to grief, and then of course there are five tests in a test match series.

Rules aside there seemed to me to be a certain symmetry in that. That there is a process, a level of commitment and engagement needed in both grief and a five test series, in order to understand and survive. As Ellen says in the play 'if we take it to the fifth stage, then that's still something.'

Grief also forces us to deal with so many of the things that as a writer I am driven to write about. Because all stories about grief must surely also be about love, loss and life, about the terrifying search to find oneself again amongst the wreckage. Grief and love are hard work, as is the re-invention of oneself in a new city. And whilst Sydney is a city of immense beauty, and one that has many treasures, at times I've found it hard, cool and impenetrable. So when I realised that I could live and maybe even be happy here, it came with the discovery that I could still live, after my loss.

As for the cricket, it is my father's favourite thing. Both as a child and an adult, as his daughter, I have watched it with him, and alone, desperately trying to get it, to make sense of it, to be closer to him. I'm closer to being there now, but I'm still a humble amateur, who's learning.

Which brings me back full circle to my first conversation with Sam at Griffin. I told him I wanted to write a romantic comedy about grief, Sydney and cricket. He did what all good artistic directors should do at that moment, he smiled and bought me another glass of wine.

So I would like to thank Sam Strong and Chris Mead for their vision, faith, friendship and collective wisdom, as well as the Griffin family for letting me tell it. I would also like to thank Shannon and our beautiful cast, Belinda, TLJ and Nathan, for giving this play life.

Jane Bodie

PLAYWRIGHT'S NOTE

Jane Bodie
Writer

For **Griffin Theatre Company**: Debut. **Other Theatre**: For PWA Festival 2011: *Music*. For Hampstead Theatre, UK: *A Single Act*, *Us*. For Theatre 503 UK: *Hallelujah*. For Soho Theatre UK: *Out of Me*. For Belvoir Company B/*59E59* New York: *Ride*. For The Storeroom: *Still*. For Trades Hall/Edinburgh Fringe: *Fourplay*. For Trades Hall/Melbourne Comedy Festival: *Speaking in Thongs*. **Television**: *The Secret Life of Us*, *CrashBurn*, *No Angels*, *Moving Wallpaper*. **Radio**: For Radio 4, UK: *The Cross*, *The Well*. For ABC Radio National: *Out of Sound*, *Seeing Somebody*, *In Glass*. **Other positions:** Head of Playwriting at NIDA (current). Royal Court Theatre's Young Writers Program 2005. **Awards**: Patrick White Playwrights' Award nomination. 2007 Victorian Premier's Literary Award (*A Single Act*). 2003 Green Room Award for Outstanding Writing (*Still*), Ewa Czajor Memorial Award nomination (director). **Training**: 2005 The National Theatre (UK) professional attachment (writer).

Shannon Murphy
Director

For **Griffin Theatre Company**: *Heartbreak Hotel*, *Crestfall*. **Other Theatre**: For Sydney Theatre Company: *Tusk Tusk*. For Belvoir B Sharp: *Bliss*, *My Name is Rachel Corrie*. For Adelaide Fringe: *The Age of Consent*. For The Old Fitzroy Theatre: *Trapture*. For NIDA: *Dutchman*, *The Love Talker*. For Flinders University: *Shoot/Get Treasure/Repeat*. For Florida Players: *Fear & Misery of the Third Reich*, *Garbage for Fuel*. As Assistant Director: For Belvoir Company B: *Gethsemane*. For Sydney Theatre Company: *Rabbit*. For Bell Shakespeare: *Taming of the Shrew*. For Belvoir B Sharp: *Jesus Hopped the 'A' Train*. **Other Positions**:

Director in Residence, Griffin Theatre Company. Emerging Artist, Virginia Stage Company. **Awards**: Sydney Theatre Award for Best Independent Production and nomination for Best Director (*My Name is Rachel Corrie*). 2010 Mike Walsh Fellowship recipient. **Training**: NIDA Director's Course. BFA Performance (Hons), University of Florida.

Brandon Martignago
Assistant Director

For Griffin Theatre Company: Debut. Other Theatre: As director: For The Street Theatre: *Hating Alison Ashley*. For GirlTalk: *Classic Claustrophobia, The Copy Room*. For DTC: *Words In The Flow Of Life*. As assistant director: For Global Creatures: *King Kong* (Workshop 1). For Queensland Theatre Company/Brisbane Festival: *Macbeth*. For Child's Play: *Alice in Wonderland, The Witches*. Film: For Sky Pictures: *Up'n'Down* (music video) Awards: Canberra Area Theatre Award – Best Director of a Play (*Hating Alison Ashley*).

Belinda Bromilow
Ellen

For **Griffin Theatre Company**: *Blood and Bone*. **Other Theatre**: For Belvoir B Sharp: *My Name is Rachel Corrie, Seven Blow Jobs*. For Sydney Theatre Company: *The Grenade, Boy Gets Girl*. For Tamarama Rock Surfers/Under the Hood Productions: *Little Boy*. For VCA Directors' Showcase: *Tattoo*. For White Wave Productions: *Whale Music*. For Company of Players: *Moving In*. For Grahamstown Festival, South Africa: *Zombie Hands*. **Film**: For 20 Something Survival Guide: *Not Suitable for Children*. For Warner Bros.: *Happy Feet*. For Rapacious Pictures: *The Rage in Placid Lake*. **Television**: For Southern Star: *Spirited*. For Seven Network: *Packed To The Rafters, All Saints*. For ITV: *Talk To Me*. For ABC TV: *MDA, Shakespeare Out Loud*. For Millennium TV: *McLeod's Daughters*. **Awards**: 2008 Sydney Theatre Awards Best Independent Production (*My Name is Rachel Corrie*). 2003 Melbourne Fringe Award for Best Show (*Ticky Tacky*). 1999 Leslie Anderson Scholarship for Best Actor, WAAPA. **Training**: WAAPA, Bachelor of Arts (Theatre and Literature), Curtin University of Technology.

Tony Llewellyn-Jones
Brian

For **Griffin Theatre Company**: Debut. **Other Theatre**: For Melbourne Theatre Company: *Tonight at 8.30, Macquarie, Forget-Me-Not-Lane, Danton's Death, How Does Your Garden Grow?, Sticks and Bones, The Plough and The Stars, The Tavern, Mother Courage, An Ideal Husband, The Cherry Orchard, The Time Is Not Yet Ripe, Paying The Piper, Batman's Beachhead, Much Ado About Nothing, You Want It Don't You Billy?, Life x 3, The Visit, Two Brothers, Realism*. For Nimrod Theatre Company: *The Tooth of Crime, Jesters, The Bacchoi, The Seagull, Kookaburra, Much Ado About Nothing, Richard III, Well Hung, The Speakers, Rockola*. For Old Tote Theatre Company: *The Matchmaker, The Norman Conquests*. For Sydney Theatre Company: *The Crucible, Saint Joan, Corporate Vibes, Life after George, King Lear, The Tempest, Amigos* and *Metamorphosis*. For Club Cockroach: *Merry Christmas Pauline Hanson*. For Marian Street: *Gone to Bali!, All Things Considered*. For Bell Shakespeare: *Henry IV, Henry V, Much Ado About Nothing*. For Belvoir B Sharp: *Homebody/Kabul*. For Belvoir Company B: *The Power of Yes*. **Film:** *Inside Looking Out, Kostas, Picnic At Hanging Rock, The Last Wave, The Girl Who Met Simone De Beauvoir In Paris, Fatty Finn, To Market To Market, Seeing Red, The Nun And The Bandit, Exile, Cosi, Human Touch, Salvation*. **Television:** *Who Do You Think You Are?, One Day Miller, Geese Mate For Life!, The Paper Boy, Blabbermouth and Stickybeak, G.P., All Saints, Backberner, CrashBurn, Blackjack, Hell Has Harbour Views, The Prime Minister Is Missing, Rogue Nation, The Last Confession of Alexander Pearce, I Spry*. **Other Positions**: Producer for Paul Cox features: *Man of Flowers, My First Wife, Cactus, Vincent: The Life and Death of Vincent Van Gogh, Salvation*. Previously Board Member of the Sydney Theatre Company, the Australian National Playwrights' Conference, St. Kilda and Melbourne Film Festivals, and National Performers Committee of Actors' Equity. **Training:** NIDA and ANU.

Nathan Lovejoy
Various

For **Griffin Theatre Company**: *Way to Heaven*. **Other Theatre**: For Bell Shakespeare: *Much Ado About Nothing*, *The Tempest*. For Bell Shakespeare/Queensland Theatre Company: *Anatomy Titus Fall of Rome*. For Sydney Theatre Company: *The Crucible*. For Sydney Symphony: *A Midsummer Night's Dream*. For Ride On Theatre/Belvoir B Sharp: *The Merchant of Venice*. For Siren Theatre Company: *Twelfth Night*. For New Black/Darlinghurst Theatre Company: *Bones*. For Harlos Productions: *King Lear*. For Keene/Taylor Theatre Project: *Homeland*. **Film**: For DreamWorks/HBO: *The Pacific*. For Arclight Films: *Storm Warning*. **Television**: For ABC: *At Home With Julia*, *My Place Part 2*, *Laid*, *Review with Myles Barlow*. For Network Seven: *Headland*. **Training**: NIDA. **Awards**: FBi Sydney Music Arts and Culture Awards, nominated for Best Performer (*Way to Heaven*).

Rita Carmody
Designer

For **Griffin Theatre Company**: *Bug, Crestfall, References to Salvador Dali Make Me Hot*. **Other Theatre:** For Riverside Theatre: *Rainbow's End* (costume). For Ensemble Theatre: *My Wonderful Day*. For Tamarama Rock Surfers: *Boxing Day, Rock Paper Scissors, Belle's Line, The Age of Consent*. For Flinders University: *Shoot/Get Treasure/ Repeat*. For ATYP: *Rio Saki and Other Falling Debris*. For Court Theatre Christchurch: *My Name is Rachel Corrie*. For Darlinghurst Theatre: *Pool (no water)*. For NORPA: *The Bloody Bride*. For Belvoir B Sharp: *Miss Julie* (costume). **Television**: *The Renovators, The Biggest Loser, Deadly Women, Behind Mansion Walls, Killer Instinct* (wardrobe department). **Other Positions**: Lecturer and Tutor in design at COFA, UNSW. **Training**: NIDA, Design Course.

Verity Hampson
Lighting Designer

For **Griffin Theatre Company:** *And No More Shall We Part*, *The Brothers Size, Angela's Kitchen, Like a Fishbone, Way to Heaven, Crestfall, References to Salvador Dali Make Me Hot, Dealing with Clair, Family Stories Belgrade, The Cold Child, Live Acts on Stage*. **Other Theatre:** For Belvoir Company B: *The Business, That Face, The Gates of Egypt*. For Sydney Theatre Company: *Hamlet, Before/*

After Leviathan, Tusk Tusk, The Comedy of Errors, The Beauty Queen of Leenane, The Accidental Death of an Anarchist, The Crucible. For Belvoir B Sharp: The Sweetest Thing, Fool for Love, Parlour Song, Bliss, Lady Macbeth of Mtsensk, Queen C, A View of Concrete, The Merchant of Venice, An Oak Tree, 2000 Feet Away, The Small Things, Pan, Duck, A Family Affair. For NORPA: Engine, The Bloody Bride, Not Like Beckett. For NYTC: Growing Up. For Darlinghurst Theatre Company: Bad Jazz, Lady Windermere's Fan, Pool (no water), Terrorism, Some Explicit Polaroid's, Breathing Corpse. For ATYP: House on Fire, Citizenship, VX 18504, Phaedra's Love, Battlegrounds. For Opera House Studio: The Colour of Panic, Monkeyshines: Kids Cabaret. For Mardi Gras: The Fabulous Punch and Judy Show, Bison, Natural Born Hooker. For Critical Stages: Wilde Tales. For Merrigong: Camarilla. **Television:** Live at the Basement. **Other Positions:** Teaching: NIDA and UNSW Nepean.

Nate Edmondson
Sound Designer
For Griffin Theatre Company: Debut. **Other Theatre:** For Red Rabbit Theatre Company: Fefu And Her Friends. For Two Birds One Stone/Darlinghurst Theatre: The Coming World. For Little Ones Theatre/Tamarama Rock Surfers: Pictures of Bright Lights. For New Theatre: Julius Caesar. For Crow-Crow Productions/Tamarama Rock Surfers: Flightfall. For NIDA Open Program: Alice In Wonderland. For NIDA: The Ugly One, Accidental Death Of An Anarchist, As You Like It, Still, The Lover. **Other Positions:** Short Film Work: Kaleidoscope (2010), Gibney's Island (2011). **Training:** NIDA Production Course (current third-year student).

Steve Francis
Composer
For Griffin Theatre Company: Speaking in Tongues, Strange Attractor. **Other Theatre:** For Belvoir Company B: The Power of Yes, The Book of Everything, Gethesmane, Man from Mukinupin, Ruben Guthrie, Baghdad Wedding, Keating!, Paul, Parramatta Girls, Capricornia, Box the Pony, In Our Name, Gulpilil, Page 8, The Spook. For Sydney Theatre Company: Bloodland, Tusk Tusk, Leviathan, Spring Awakening, The Removalists, Rabbit, Pig Iron People, Gallipoli, The Great, Romeo and

Juliet, The Taming of the Shrew, Embers, The 7 Stages of Grieving, Fat Pig, A Hard God, Stolen. Riverside Theatre: *Rainbow's End.* Bell Shakespeare: *Romeo and Juliet.* **Other Positions:** For dance, *Belong, Fire, True Stories, Skin, Corroboree, Walkabout, Bush, Boomerang* (Bangarra Dance Theatre), *Totem* (The Australian Ballet). Produced and co-composed music for *Awakenings*, the Indigenous section of the Sydney Olympic Games Opening Ceremony, *Earth* for the Rugby World Cup Opening. **Film:** *Mr Patterns, Box, Black Talk, Djarn Djarns.* **TV:** *Dangerous, Double Trouble, Macumba, Picture the Women.* **Awards:** 2003 Helpmann Awards for Best Original Score and Best New Australian Work for *Walkabout.*

Isabella Kerdijk
Stage Manager

For **Griffin Theatre Company**: *And No More Shall We Part*, New Writers Festival. **Other Theatre**: For Ensemble Theatre: *Rainman, The Ruby Sunrise* (Assistant Stage Manager). For First Stage Productions: *Woman.* For Legs on the Wall: *Bubble* (Assistant Stage Manager). For NIDA Open Program, *A Midsummer Night's Dream.* **Other Positions**: For The Garden of Unearthly Delights: *Spiegel Tent* (Venue Manager). Sydney Festival, Woodford Folk Festival, Puppetry of the Penis (Production Manager). **Training**: NIDA.

Griffin Theatre Company

Griffin Theatre Company is Australia's leading new writing theatre and the home of the best Australian stories.

Formed in 1978, Griffin took up residence at the SBW Stables Theatre in 1980. For over 30 years since, the Company has been the boutique powerhouse of Australian theatre: consistently breaking new ground and making an outstanding contribution to the national culture.

Griffin has always been the place to make a great start. Australia's most loved and performed play – Michael Gow's *Away* – premiered at Griffin. The hit films *Lantana* and *The Boys* also began life as plays first produced by the company, as did the TV series *Heartbreak High*. Many artists who now contribute significantly to the Australian theatre, film and television industries began professional careers at Griffin, including Cate Blanchett, Jacqueline McKenzie and David Wenham.

In recent years, this success has continued with smash hits like *Angela's Kitchen* and *Speaking In Tongues*, and return seasons and national and international tours of plays including *Savage River*, *The Story of the Miracles at Cookie's Table*, *Mr Bailey's Minder* and *Holding the Man*.

Now, Griffin is the only professional theatre company in Sydney entirely dedicated to the development and production of new Australian plays. Presenting four or five productions each year, Griffin regularly tours across Australia. The company also acts as a hub for artists and audiences alike; co-presenting the best Independent theatre in Sydney through Griffin Independent; providing audiences with diverse and innovative experiences through Griffringe and Griffin Between the Lines events; nurturing the theatre-makers of tomorrow through our education program, the Griffin Ambassadors; and harnessing the talents of the country's best emerging writers and directors through our groundbreaking resident artist scheme, the Griffin Studio.

Griffin aims to develop and stage the best new Australian stories, in the most exciting theatre in the country, for the widest possible audience.

Griffin Theatre Company

13 Craigend St, Kings Cross NSW 2011
Phone: 02 9332 1052
Fax: 02 9331 1524
Email: info@griffintheatre.com.au
Web: griffintheatre.com.au

SBW Stables Theatre

10 Nimrod St
Kings Cross NSW 2011
Online bookings at griffintheatre.com.au
or call 02 9361 3817

ABOUT GRIFFIN

In 2010, we teamed up with our pals at Tonkin Zulaikha Greer to give the SBW Stables Theatre a well-earned renovation.

So far we've seen the Stables foyer get a much needed facelift and 2011 saw work start on the auditorium, including a re-fit to the theatre itself, making the seating much more comfy to enjoy shows from and improving backstage spaces, making the lives of our hardworking stage managers and actors that bit easier.

Tonkin Zulaikha Greer are not only a perfect fit for the job with their experience working on a multitude of historically and culturally significant sites, but have also been integral for their vision and their generosity as sponsors of the project.

But TZG aren't the only ones who've been generous; we've had a groundswell of support for the project from theatre fans all around the country and we're so grateful!

But there is yet even still more work to do – Stage 3 of our capital works project will look at some significant changes that will open the foyer up with a new north-facing entrance, improving access and airflow, and accommodating a new bar and cafe.

We will also make a significant investment in an ongoing program, How Green Are We, to make our theatre more sustainable.

If you'd like to help finish the job, give our Development Manager, Allie Townsend, a call on (02) 9332 1052 or drop her a line at philanthropy@griffintheatre.com.au. Donors at brick level and above will be acknowledged in perpetuity in the foyer.

Beam ($120,000+)
Seaborn, Broughton & Walford Foundation

Pillar ($45,000)
Bluptons
Ros Horin & Joe Skrzynski
Rockend Technology Pty Ltd
ArtsNSW
Rebel Penfold-Russell
Kim Williams

CAPITAL WORKS PROGRAM

Step ($15,000)
Antoinette Albert
Nathan Bennett & Nick Marchand
Charmaine & Michael Bradley
Lewin Family
Ezekiel Solomon
Stuart Thomas
Townsend Family

Brick ($3,000)
Anonymous (1)
Gina Bowman, Sally Noonan & Mark Sutcliffe
Baker & McKenzie
BOSE
Gillian Appleton
John Bell & Anna Volska
Jo Briscoe & Brenna Hobson
Rob Brookman & Verity Laughton
Actors Centre Australia
Bob & Helena Carr
Ange Cecco & Melanie Bienemann
Rae & Russ Cottle
Glyn Cryer
Thonet Australia
Alison Deans & Kevin Powell
Richard Glover
Peter Graves, Canberra
Maurice Green AM & Christina Green
The Griffins – Allie, Bel, Jas & Jen
Larry & Tina Grumley
Catherine Hastings
Baly Douglass Foundation
Mary & John Holt
Ken & Lilian Horler
Chris Jackman
Currency Press
Peter, Angela & Piper Keel
Brett Boardman & Lee Lewis
Lisa Mann Creative Management
Wendy McCarthy AO
Sophie McCarthy & Tony Green
Bruce Meagher & Greg Waters
Dr David Nguyen
Dianne O'Connell
Peter O'Connell
Debra Oswald
Anthony Paull
Ian Phipps
Peace of Mind Technology
Celina Pront
Joel Pront
Nicki Bloom & Geordie Brookman
Chris Puplick AM
Chris & Fran Roberts
Ian Robertson
Mike Robinson
Cre8ion
Will Sheehan
Kate & David Sheppard
Diana Simmonds
Smith & Jones
Augusta Supple
Chris Tooher & Rebecca Tinning

Current as at 15 September 2011

Patron Seaborn, Broughton and
Walford Foundation
Board Michael Bradley (Chair), Hilary Bell,
Damian Borchok, Lisa Lewin (Treasurer),
Sophie McCarthy, Leigh O'Neill, Sam Strong
and Stuart Thomas

Artistic Director Sam Strong
General Manager Simon Wellington
Finance Manager Alison Baly
Production Manager Micah Johnson
Artistic Associate Belinda Kelly
Marketing Manager Jennifer Cannock
Development Manager Allie Townsend
Front-of-House Manager Jasmine De Carlo
Associate Director/Literary Advisor Lee Lewis
Affiliate Directors James Dalton and
Kai Raisbeck
Griffin Studio Ian Meadows, Kate Mulvany,
Shannon Murphy, Paige Rattray
PlayWriting Australia Residency
Vanessa Bates, Jessica Bellamy, Victoria
Haralabidou and Jessica Redenbach

Writers under commission
A PlayWriting Australia Co-Commission
Jane Bodie *(This Year's Ashes)*

Web Developer House of Laudanum
Brand and Graphic Design Interbrand
Photography Michael Corridore
Printing Whirlwind

Griffin Foundation
The price of a ticket to a show at Griffin
actually only covers 23% of the real costs.
This leaves an ever increasing gap for us to
fill through government funding, sponsorship
and the generosity of our individual supporters.
Your support helps us to bridge the gap and
keep ticket prices affordable while keeping
our work at its best. To make a donation and
a difference, contact Griffin on 9332 1052 or
donate online at www.griffintheatre.com.au.

GRIFFIN
STAFF &
DONORS

Production ($10,000)
Anonymous (2)
Estate of the late Ruth Barratt

Studio ($5,000)
Gil Appleton
The Goodness Foundation
Tony Green
Richard & Elizabeth Longes
Sophie McCarthy
Leigh O'Neill
Sam Strong and Katherine Slattery

Workshop ($1,000–$4,999)
Baly Douglass Foundation
Richard Cottrell
Ros & Paul Espie
Thomas & Ingeborg Girgensohn
John & Mary Holt
Stephen Manning
Jane Martin
Peter & Dianne O'Connell
Anthony Paull
Geoff & Wendy Simpson
Judy & Sam Weiss
Paul & Jennifer Winch

Reading ($500–$999)
Anonymous (1)
Wendy Ashton
Nick Goldsmith
Jennifer Ledgar & Bob Lim
Mark O'Neill
Isla Tooth
Leslie Walford
Dr Bill Winspear AM

First Draft ($200–$499)
Anonymous (2)
Jes Andersen
Jason Bourne
Wendy Buswell
Alex Byrne
Corinne Campbell
Michael & Colleen Chesterman
Amanda Clark
Victor Cohen & Rosie McColl
Max Dingle
Eric Dole
Wendy Elder
Elizabeth Evatt
Gadens Lawyers
Nicky Gluyas
David & Christine Hartgill
Belinda Hazelton
Janet Heffernan
Henry Johnston
Margaret Johnson
Michala Lander
Caroline Le Plastrier
Christopher McCabe
Duncan McKay
Frances Milat
Neville Mitchell
Mullinars Casting Consultants
Natalie Pelham
Alex-Oonagh Redmond
Annabel Ritchie
Rebecca Rocheford-Davies
Andrew Rosenberg
Diane & David Russell
Ros Tarszisz
Nicholas & Elise Yates
William Zappa

Current as at 15 September 2011

Griffin would like to thank the following

Patron

Griffin acknowledges the generosity of the Seaborn, Broughton and Walford Foundation in allowing it, since 1986, the use of the SBW Stables Theatre rent free, less outgoings.

2011 Season Sponsors

Interbrand

JCDecaux

Production Sponsor

holding
redlich
lawyers

Monday Rush Sponsor

FOXTEL

Associate Sponsors

MAR/QUE

tonkin
greer
ARCHITECTS

OTTO RISTORANTE

PKF
Chartered Accountants
& Business Advisers

Company Sponsors

SIGNWAVE
NEWTOWN

CURRENCY
PRESS

Rosenfeld,
Kant & Co.
Business & Financial Solutions

EIGHT HOTELS
— AUSTRALIA —
Boutique Hotel Collection

TimeOut
Sydney
timeout.com/sydney

thewinesociety

V & R
THE VICTORIA ROOM
BAR RESTAURANT

WHIRLWIND
More than ink on paper

Foundations and Trusts

bourke street bakery

UNSW
THE UNIVERSITY OF NEW SOUTH WALES

Government Sponsors

Australian Government

Australia Council for the Arts

NSW Communities
arts nsw

CITY OF SYDNEY

Griffin Theatre Company is assisted by the Australian Government through the Australia Council, its arts funding and advisory body and the NSW Government through Arts NSW.

GRIFFIN
SPONSORS